Changing Lives

Voices from a School that Works

Jane Day

Preface by Deborah W. Meier
Remarks by Emanuel Pariser
Photographs by Maryanne Mott and Jane Day

UNIVERSITY
PRESS OF
AMERICA

Lanham • New York • London

Copyright © 1994 by
University Press of America,® Inc.
4720 Boston Way
Lanham, Maryland 20706

3 Henrietta Street
London WC2E 8LU England

Library of Congress Cataloging-in-Publication Data

Day, Jane.
Changing lives : voices from a school that works / by Jane Day ;
preface by Deborah W. Meier ; remarks by Emanuel Pariser ;
photographs by Maryanne Mott and Jane Day.
p. cm.
1. Community School (Camden, Me.) – Students – Biography.
2. Socially handicapped children – Education (Secondary) –
Maine – Camden – Biography. 3. High school students –
Maine – Camden – Biography. I. Title.
LD7501.C227D39 373.741'53—dc20 93–39244 CIP

ISBN 0–8191–9419–0 (pbk. : alk. paper)

 The paper used in this publication meets the minimum requirements of
American National Standard for Information Sciences—Permanence
of Paper for Printed Library Materials, ANSI Z39.48–1984.

For these young people
who bared their lives with honesty and courage
that others may find hope and take heart.

Contents

Foreword

And then they lived happily ever after.

I realized recently that we weep with joy at our children's weddings—even after we have outgrown fairy tales—because we long to believe there will be someone there for them when we no longer are. Someone to kiss away the bruises, to stand up for them, to nurse them when they are ill and defenseless. Yet we know better; what they really need is the competence and the will to overcome.

We teachers have "teacherly" dreams much like our "parently" ones. The common thread is our hope that something we do will make a difference in our children's lifelong capacity to cope with the challenges, travails, and crises that will inevitably come their way. Whether we teach history or math or just teach children, we see our work as sharing the passions that help us to survive.

I call this quality resiliency rather than toughness. It comes from a determination to enjoy life, or at least to make the most of it. It is the flat refusal to break, even if one must bend quite low.

Can we teach it? Not exactly, but when our teaching is going right, resiliency permeates the school, the passing conversations, the quality of relationships, the kind of demands made, and the nature of the rites of passage devised.

Central Park East (CPE) once interviewed its elementary school graduates ten years later. They agreed with C-Schoolers Brenda, "It's not about getting a high-school diploma," and Aaron, "If you toss aside all the academics, this would still be a great school." Still, the students of both schools get their high-school diplomas; they get the job done. The C-School and CPE are demanding.

Something happens at the C-School in Camden that nurtures passion, enhances whatever resiliency these wounded teens bring with them. In the short six months habits take root that bear fruit over time.

When I started reading these tales, I expected fairy stories with magic endings: youngsters coming in troubled—abused, abusive, lost—and leaving on a never-faltering trajectory of success. Of course then I could have cynically dismissed the book as so much public relations or alternately wondered enviously why it has been my misfortune never to have hit upon such a magic cure for those I love. The truth is, six months is a short time. Some kids attend CPE from the age of 5 to 12; others start at 12 and stay until 18. Some spend only a year or two; others stick with us for all 12 years. The C-School has just 6 months, but it is clearly long enough to plant deeply a seed that keeps growing.

Almost every story is bittersweet. Almost all falter—some rather badly—over and over. Life is mostly rough on them, before and after. Few come from families or communities that are doing well. The kids are trying to break patterns of failure that stretch out behind them, bleak histories of alcohol, drugs, unemployment, divorce, and physical violence.

What shines through is that they have developed the habit of being unsentimentally reflective. Their inward look includes a startling willingness to take responsibility for their own lives. There is no hint of grievance-collecting, not a whiney tone in the lot, not even a legitimate sense of self-pity! They have a past to tell about and a way of thinking it over that does not lack for psychological insight. Their way of putting the pieces together gives them strength, endurance, and a confidence that they'll resurface if they hold on to two unshakable beliefs: the power of intelligent thought and the importance of being responsible.

"You pick up your pieces, correct your mistakes," says Tony. According to Steve, "Life is a real big challenge to me, and I feel that I'm aware of a lot more than a person who didn't have any problems in the first place. In a way, I feel real lucky." The two themes—reflectiveness and responsibility—emerge over and over.

Yes, it's a place of family and caring, but what is remarkable is that these are not stories of the redemptive power of love and family life but the redemptive power of work, of taking responsibility for one's own condition. This is the way it is; these are the rules of the game. The teachers care, but unlike family they make demands—paying the rent, getting to work on time, and cooking. These are the details that count. Over and over. Day in and day out.

At the toughest times in my life—when struck by the death of loved ones, betrayals by friends and lovers, financial crises—such daily details helped me recover. I was grateful that I had to do the laundry, make dinner, and get to work everyday. Like the discovery I made last year: If I keep my eyes on the trail and take small steady steps, I can walk a bit farther than I think; in fact, I can walk almost forever.

At CPE we have replaced the metaphor of "school as family" with "school as community." We try to remember that it's not our job to be good parents, although all grown-ups are parental at times just as all parents are "teacherly." To pretend is to offer another injury, another betrayal. What's necessary is to nurture the strength that's there, the capacity for success, the will to finish. "I succeeded," says Aaron of the first time he did "what I set out to do." "It allowed me to complete something," says Jeanine.

It's not an accident that the School founders and co-directors, Emanuel Pariser and Dora Lievow, called it the Community School. It's not family, although it's close. But precisely in the difference lies its strength. "The staff have a strange way," says Aaron, "of being your friend and your teacher." "I took them as sort of halfway between authority figures and peers," says Ed. "They are my chosen family," says Judy as she describes a community that kicked her out, "daring to confront me by saying 'That's not acceptable,'" but then took her back, all the while feeding her books, nourishing her passion for literature.

"There was an environment...that nurtured self-thought," says Pat. "I had much more freedom...but with...responsibility. What you do not only affects yourself but other people—that's the big thing I learned." She acknowledges the toughness but also the need to "take what you are given and mold it into something that makes you happy." Angie refers to that sense of "forever giving us choices," but in the very next sentence she talks about responsibility. Says Dwayne, "The turning point for me that really opened my eyes was about responsibility. That really sunk in....You got to grow up and smell the coffee."

One after another they come back to these themes. For some it was also a real home, a place of deep personal attachments. But even when that was less true, they honored the experience for its demands. Now they think about their lives and act responsibly.

Behind these stories are the people who work at the School. It's not just that they are patient, as the kids note so often. It's that they really like the kids they get—adolescents full of energy and rebelliousness, experts at getting away with things and being angry and persistently noncompliant. These intellectually lively grown-ups with strong standards and values, keen senses of responsibility, passions for the world, and skills of their own enjoy these kids. They are adults worth knowing. They know "you can be intelligent, but you don't have to be orthodox," as Jeanine put it.

Perhaps the magic is that the youngsters sense they are for the first time amidst adults who enjoy them and don't want them to become someone else. These strong-minded value-laden adults like them even when they "just have to be me" with all the baggage that comes with it. Their families love them as much, probably in most cases more, however ineptly. I have often reminded myself of this as I dealt with parents for what appeared to be thoughtlessness, cruelty, and self-absorption. Parents too have a story to tell.

The kids seem occasionally embarrassed at how close and strong the bonds are, how much they mean to these otherwise tough-minded adults. Maybe the 6-month limit helps because not one kid seems to worry that the bonds will prove dangerous to the tasks that lay ahead. Maybe they dare give so much because the time limits are clear and short.

These young people didn't leave the Community School to live happily ever after, any more than our own children do. But they have an anchor; they learned something that took many of us far longer to discover about the power of being competent at the tasks of living—paying the electric bill as well as having a love for living and recognizing the importance of thoughtfulness and responsibility. With such "simple" tools, they will endlessly invent and reinvent their lives.

—Deborah W. Meier

Introduction

This book holds the stories of forty individuals who became adults the hard way. As teenagers some were in trouble with the law, others with drugs. Many were alienated from their families, and all had left or been told to leave school before they graduated.

With the help of friends, social workers, probation officers, caring guidance counselors, or family members, they found the Community School and despite sometimes disabling fears attempted to complete their high-school education. Now adults in their twenties and thirties, many have children and are living meaningful and responsible lives.

As a teacher and friend, I continue to learn from each of these graduates. They inspire me. In my own struggles to change and grow, I marvel at their tremendous courage and determination.

In twenty years the School has worked with 241 students who have stayed for two or more months. For this book we selected one from those who did not finish the School's six-month term and the rest from the 180 students who did. A recent ten-year evaluation demonstrated that students entering the program did not have a hopeful future: Only 37% came from intact families, 66% had some form of criminal justice involvement, and 83% self-reported moderate to excessive drug use.

What kind of influence could a six-month, residential, alternative school exert on the disrupted lives of these youngsters? Our latest statistics indicate that 179 students have earned a Community School high-school diploma; since leaving, 45 have gone on to formal education or training, and 15 into the military; 100% have held jobs of some sort and 90% are self-supporting; 75% with prior incarceration records did not recidivate; 11% were incarcerated or adjudicated; and 20% have been involved with recovery programs.

Dora Lievow and I started the School fresh out of our own adolescence in the sixties. We wanted to impart our interest and joy in life to others. Our school was born of the desire to create a community of learners where people could be themselves rather than fit the conventional roles of teacher and student.

The School's simple central format has remained constant through the years: Students work in the community and pay room and board; they are individually tutored and take a series of competency exams; and they live in a self-governing community of students and staff which challenges them to trust and participate. Staff decision-making is democratic.

When we began in 1973, the era of free schools was coming to an end. Politically minded educators like Jonathan Kozol saw private alternatives as middle-class options which failed to address the major problems plaguing American education. The general public was paying little attention to the fact that every year 25% of high-school students in America were not graduating.

Twenty years later we still have a national dropout rate of 25% which means a million teenagers will leave school in 1993 without graduating. The costs associated with dropping out are phenomenal. The problem is generational as evidenced by the fact that the most predictive indicator that a student will drop out of school continues to be the mother's educational level.

Obviously, the Community School has not had a noticeable impact on national dropout rates. We have not worked at the School to change this statistic. We have worked with individuals to help reach a goal that they despaired of ever reaching, to reintroduce them to the experience of community and responsibility. If we are able to continue our work for another twenty years, perhaps statistics even more important than the dropout rate—such as the percentage of children who grow up in abusive homes—will change.

Pulling together the interviews and photography sessions for this book has encouraged me. I was not sure what we would find when we looked closely at the adults these teenagers had become. Would they be working? In abusive relationships? Continuing their education? Abusing drugs and alcohol? In jail?

Although by no means perfect, our graduates' lives are proof that we have been on the right track, that our very personal brand of education has had its effect. Our students are now raising their children in more intelligent and caring ways. They are breaking educational barriers which have existed within their families for generations.

I hope this book shows that solutions to problems need not match the scale of the problems themselves. We need to pay less attention to overwhelming numbers and more attention to the individuals who comprise those numbers. When asked how she planned to deal with the millions of people in need that her order had not yet helped, Mother Teresa replied, "one by one."

There are three people without whose efforts this work would never have seen the light of day. Jane Day, who interviewed each graduate and spent days and nights bringing their stories to life on the printed page, was the first person to write an article on the School when she was editor of the local newspaper. Her ability to truly represent what these students had to say and to stay with her subjects rather than analyze them has been remarkable. Our photographer, Maryanne Mott, joined us early in the process, diving fearlessly into a community she did not know. The donation of her time, materials, and expertise gave the project its striking visual aspect. Much of who these youngsters have become is etched plainly and honestly on their faces, which Maryanne has lovingly captured on film. Finally, every joint venture needs someone to make sure that everything is in the right place at the right time. Maybe Marty King didn't know what she was signing on for when she joined us to copyedit and lay out the book, but she assumed that position for the final stretch. Her contribution added immeasurably to the quality and symmetry of this book; without it we would have missed our first deadline and probably several following ones.

Thanks are also due to Community School staff—Bob Dickens, Cindy Olsen, Buck O'Herin, Bonnie Versboncouer, Huldah Warren, Fran Wheeler, Agnes Beloniasz, Barbara Robidoux, Rhett Hutto, Peter Stewart, and especially Dora Lievow who had to pick up the most slack and always remained eager to proofread and respond to the material—who gave me the occasional time off to work on it; to Deborah Meier for her moving and personal foreward; to my sons Elijah and Eben who put up with the craziness at home in the last few weeks before the deadline; to my brother David, who has given me confidence in my own writing; to Frank Antonucci, Director, Maine Office of Dropout, Truant, and Alternative Education; Herb Kohl; Bill Ayers; and our National Advisory Board, particularly Dr. Julius Richmond, Kitty Lustman Findling, and Rushworth Kidder, who encouraged me every step of the way on this long journey.

Without the generous contributions of The Seymour Lustman Trust, The Bay Foundation, the John Anson Kittridge Fund, Neil and Sheila Welliver, and Caroline and Wayne Morong, this book would never have been written. Finally, I must thank the students who participated in this project and allowed us to ask the hard questions and take the intimidating photographs. It is, after all, their book.   —Emanuel Pariser

Defining Ourselves, Defining a Program

1973 - 1978

The Community School began with an explosion: On August 1, 1973, the director of the Redington Pond School (RPS) in Rangeley, Maine, fired us as directors of the Sea School, its newly established Camden branch, and told us to return all the equipment and students immediately. On August 15 we formally created the Community School.

Redington Pond was a year-round camp which adapted Outward Bound theory by having kids from Boston, Providence, and their suburbs live in the Maine woods for an extended time through winter and summer. In a letter to a former professor of mine I wrote, "The Sea School will take kids with the outdoor experience of RPS and gear them back to life in the city. We will try to develop a sense of internal community as well as a sense of responsibility to the external one....we will develop urban survival skills."

Upon learning that our services were no longer needed, I threw the phone across the room. We had invested six months in setting up the program, were deeply involved in the lives of our five students, and held outside jobs to pay the bills. Dora Lievow and I were 23 and 21 respectively and had just begun a relationship with each other.

Our teaching was based on a simple premise: We wanted our students to enjoy life the way we did and hoped that by using ourselves as models they would see the joy and value in the things we found important such as gardening, playing music, and discussing ideas, feelings, politics, philosophy, and psychology. We loved living and working with our students.

From August to January we designed and ran the Community School with the help of our consultant Bill Panton, a marriage and family counselor. It was a small operation: Dora, myself, and one student, Tom Dilibero, who had previously run away from RPS.

Catapulted from being counselors within a program to being The Program, we realized nothing would happen if we didn't do it. There were no fallback positions. I recorded these questions in my logbook at the time: "What do we mean by the word school? Is it correct to assume that our students will learn primarily by following our life-style? If there has to be more structure and we have to be authorities, will the School become less of a home and a family for all of us?"

While we struggled with these questions Bill consistently posed to us in our weekly staff meetings, Tom, Dora, and I held outside jobs to pay the rent and food bills. Pooling our money equally, we worked with Tom in the evenings on his high-school equivalency exam. Our private and professional lives were indistinguishable.

To attract students, generate funding, and get a license of some sort, we had to define ourselves to the outside world. Following the RPS model of working with delinquents and state wards, we decided to work with high-school dropouts.

A note in my log from January explains that we hoped to "force them to take control of their lives and determine their own course of action....teach them how to choose by providing a total educational environment in which incidental learning and the integration of school and work can take place....act as a source of feedback to students, indicating what is acceptable and what is not."

But most of our students came to us convinced that the adult world was untrustworthy. Making choices was useless because "plans always fall through." They felt they were second-class citizens because they had dropped out of school. When they were allowed to make choices, they often behaved self-destructively. They wanted to party and have sex and blamed their failure to succeed on authorities in their lives. Making a commitment to anything was a tremendously painful process for them.

In our first nine months Tom made it clear that he did not come to the School solely to learn how to make choices and become part of a community. He wanted a high-school diploma, not a GED, which is awarded to out-of-school and older students who pass a standardized national test. We couldn't grant him a diploma until we got approved as a school, so with the help of Blaire McCracken, the Curriculum Director at the Maine Department of Education and Cultural Services (now the Department of Education), we created an approved curriculum that combined the GED with work, residential life, and personal management. Two years after he started, Tom was granted the School's first diploma.

In those days the program was extremely fluid. People came and went rapidly. Students did not buy into the system as we had set it up. Although there were curfews, it was not uncommon for them to be out all night. As quickly as we drew lines, they stepped over them. At one point we were forced to throw out two-thirds (two students) of the student body.

We vacillated on how to share authority. Sometimes we made rules out of thin air to apply to new and unforeseen disasters; sometimes we shared decision making with the students and then became infuriated when they outvoted us. In February of 1974 I wrote, "We could operate this boat for a long while, but as my brother aptly puts it, 'The nature of your work is 80 to 90 percent bailing-out activity.'"

Despite the continuing drama and travail, students who had never passed a test succeeded. Their faces changed; they began to look better; they developed positive relationships with adults in the community; they wrote at length in the School logbooks. They were interesting human beings, not "bricks in the wall" as public school systems had made them feel. For the first time hope and possibility were quietly entering their lives.

While our house on Cross Street continued to be the center of activity, the students spent most of their time—as they do now—at work sites in the community. In the early seventies they were eligible for many jobs through CETA, a federal program. A few, like Patty and Tom, found unsubsidized jobs with local craftsmen and companies. Classes were held upstairs in the Camden YMCA, and once a month the entire School went on a challenging camping trip.

Just after we accepted our first group of students—a state ward, two probationers, and two middle-class dropouts—for a six-month term, Camden's Zoning Board refused us permission to move into the Washington Street house that Tony and Mary Bok of Camden had bought for us. Our first major grant—from the Law Enforcement and Assistance Agency—was contingent on a larger building, and our lease was up at Cross Street. The School was closed in February of 1974 with no place to go. The School's Board hired a lawyer who appealed the decision to the District Court.

With the help of a cross-section of the community vehemently opposed to the town's denial of our new residence, the program was relocated to a building in a business zone on Route 1 owned by the Congregational Church. We received our grant and for the first time were paid for our work. We hired one full-time staff and then a second. Funded primarily as a delinquency-prevention program, we took the bulk of our students out of the criminal justice system.

Although our students came by their own choice, their difficulties — substance abuse, unhealthy sexual relationships, fear of success, and fear of intimacy—remained excruciating. The house was often in upheaval;

students came home drunk, refused to meet requirements, and broke rules with abandon. We lived with the haunting sense that the School needed its students more than the students needed the School.

But by 1976 we had funding, two more full-time staff, and a track record: We had worked with 17 kids, 7 of whom had gotten their diplomas. The program was more stable and ran more independently of Dora and me. We no longer lived in full-time and began to develop an existence separate from the School.

To address the tremendous student turnover and upheaval which we experienced from term to term, we considered a three-stage model in which the School would be the second stage preceded by an outdoors experience and followed by an aftercare program. This way, we reasoned, students would be more prepared when they arrived and feel less cut off when they had to leave.

In 1977 the School won the zoning case and moved to its current home—a cozy three-story wooden-frame family residence. Former students were returning to tell us that the experience had been valuable for them. Three students who had not completed their requirements during the six-month residency had stayed in the area to do so. Although I commented in my log, "We have devised a process which brings people close enough together to want to be apart," a supportive community had formed around the School, and we became confident our work had value.   —EP

Tom Dilibero

Tom Dilibero is a slight, soft-spoken man of middle height with well-trimmed dark hair and olive skin. His eyes, a light gray brown, are gentle and expressive. He's so accustomed to being clean shaven that he felt too uncomfortable to be photographed for this interview with a weekend stubble of beard.

Tom's name is on the door of his office in the family optical business in Providence, Rhode Island, where he has worked for nine years. He lives alone in a nice apartment and works long hours, conscious of the responsibility he bears as member of a big family operation. But even now, after 18 years, when he talks about his feelings for the Community School, his eyes grow moist and redden a bit.

Tom's experience at the Community School bears symbolic resemblance to a twin birth—his own and the School's. As the School's first graduate he was witness to and participant in the pain and joy and apprehension that marks every birth. The first term had just begun when the School was abruptly severed from its parent organization and all financial support. It was a desperate time for staff and students, especially for Tom.

"I just got straightened out, and now the wall was caving in again. All I could picture was jail again. And I wasn't going back there and watch guys my age getting screwed in the ass by the guards.

"Dora and Emanuel were like on their own with a house full of kids. They put their heads together and said, 'Look, do we still want to do this?' I think everybody said yes. I know I did. It was a great opportunity. Here you are, washed up on drugs, your brain is all fizzed. All you know is pot and sex and not getting anywhere. Here you have an opportunity to have a start, a second beginning.

"I don't think anybody realizes they did it from scratch. We had this little house on Cross Street, and everybody pitched in like a family to pay for the rent. I remember working at a fruit stand down the road, and my first paycheck went towards that station wagon."

Tom considers his best job during the term was working for Chaitanya York, an organic gardener. He learned how to cultivate plants, paint a house, and build a stone wall. "To be getting that kind of experience and getting paid for it, you enjoyed going to work."

Camping and mountain climbing were fresh experiences in his life, and he entered into these activities with an enthusiasm he had never known. In retrospect he says it was part of getting serious about education and saying, "To hell with drugs and still have a good time on a camping trip.

"There were rules: no weapons, no drugs. You had chores, and you had to be loyal to your chores or pay consequences. Granted, if you'd find someone who had a joint, you'd puff a joint, but I didn't do that too much. Basically, the School made you a little more conscious of yourself—what you should and should not be doing. It did make you turn away from hard drugs and pills and stuff. It made you not want it, really, because it would interfere with studying. Going from shit to trying to get your act straightened out, you not only wanted to do it, you had to do it."

Despite his best intentions, Tom left the C-School for a couple of months over what in retrospect he terms a "stupid argument," but he was allowed to return and finish the term. Like many other former students, he hung around Camden for several months after graduation before returning home, and he established a good relationship with his parents for the first time in many years.

Tom was the rebel in a family of three boys and three girls. His parents were Italian with conservative values and lived in an upper-middle-class neighborhood of Providence. From first grade through junior high Tom went to private school which he found too strict for his liking. He wanted to go to public school because all his friends went there.

In his last year of junior high when he was about 12 or 13, he started doing drugs. "Pot, pills—experimenting. I got into it out of curiosity but mostly depression. I couldn't handle my father's rules." He lasted a year and three months at public high school. The school's drug rating was one of the worst in the country. "It was like crazy: substitute teachers smoking pot in the smoking area, people dealing drugs right in front of the principal's eyes. It was a bad place."

Tom was in and out of his family home and before long was getting into trouble. "Assaults, pot, not the normal stuff a kid that young should be in trouble for. I can see breaking a street light, but drugs? Getting in trouble with the cops?"

One night at a friend's house he overdosed on drugs. "They said I died three times." Next morning he took a handful of pills—downers—and before he knew it, he was locked up in jail. "I was 15 or 16. In jail all you see is a lot of guys older than you, and all you learn how to do is steal, pimp, and crazy things. You see a lot of traumatic things like the guards raping a kid your own age. Stuff like that does a number on your head when you're that young."

After eight months in jail waiting for trial, he got a three-year sentence. The judge gave him a choice of a correctional institution or an Outward-Bound-type school in the Maine woods. "Back in those days there was more bad stuff happening in jails or in these rehab centers than on the streets. I said, 'I'll take up in Maine.'"

Tom went to Redington Pond School where he met Dora Lievow, a member of the staff. On his first home pass—his first in over a year—Tom drank beer and smoked some pot, "but I did not stick any needles in my arm." His parents feared he had and informed the school. When the head of the school meted out punishment, Tom left for Rhode Island. He arrived after bumming rides for three days in the rain, a runaway now warranted on a police report.

He connected with a kid who had a place to stay. The two of them got jobs and soon bought an old school bus that they fitted out and moved into. "We had music in each bedroom, paneling in the hallway, stove, refrigerator—the whole bit." Tom did not contact his parents or let anyone know where he was living.

"I had more freedom than any kid my age in town. They were still living off their parents, and here I am, tons of girlfriends, tons of money, my own house on wheels. I was a little king."

One day an old friend ran into him in the park and told him his father was in the hospital and about to have heart surgery. Tom hadn't seen his father in two years and still harbored bitterness and hatred toward him, but at his roommate's urging he went to see him. He remembers it as a sad reunion.

Tom returned to the school bus and his good paying job, "but upstairs I wasn't getting anywhere. I was still on the run, still wanted. I was living under a fake name, a fake ID, and all that crap, and I got fed up with it."

In the meantime, the Sea School under the aegis of Redington Pond was starting up in Camden with some familiar staff members. At the request of Tom's parents, two staffers from the school went to Rhode Island to try to find him. They left a message urging Tom to call them with a kid in a park who knew where Tom was.

"So I called, and I was breaking up in tears. It was like, 'You actually want me to come up and start school again?' I couldn't believe the offer. I had to jump on it. I was sick of being on the run." The school took care of Tom's legal problems, and Dora went to Rhode Island to make the arrangements with the court. Tom talked with the judge who found it hard to believe that a kid his age could have lived the way he had for nine months undetected.

"I couldn't get it out at the ten-year reunion. Somehow being the first graduate I didn't want anybody to think I was a big shot making my own little speech. But when I think of the Community School, I think of Dora and Emanuel. You could tell they cared for you sort of like a nurse. They wanted you to get better, not just because it was their job, but you felt they cared, and you knew it.

"And another thing I wanted to say at the reunion: Sometimes when you're down and out and can't do it for your boss or your mother or father and you're having a bad-ass day and feel like killing yourself or whatever, I just stop and think of Dora and Emanuel and do it for them. They probably are thinking of you, and you don't even know it. They think of all their old students, but not everybody thinks they do.

"Hey, I was a brat; they were the parents I didn't have back then. Maybe I was too close to them in a way. You could feel the bond. They didn't want to see you just get your diploma; they wanted to see you become a good person instead of a fucked-up, drug-infested little bastard. I'll never forget the day I called up Emanuel and told him I was accepted to college. His voice was cracking up. I think it did a lot for him."

Pat McLellan

M and M Graphics is a bright, colorful shop. Four-color samples of the small company's design work are tacked on the walls and strewn here and there on file cabinets and desks. Along the west wall, sliding glass doors open onto a ground-level deck where several mallards waddle up the grassy slope from the Union River for crumbs.

Pat McLellan and her business partner, Louise Mechaley, work side by side at desks cluttered with artwork and proofs and pots of pens and brushes. Pat, her thin, merry face offset by oversized glasses, is on the phone with one customer after another. A bowl of soup on her desk gets cold, and Louise and two women employees joke about her skipping lunch again. It is a harmonious shop that started with a small loan, a rented camera, and plenty of spirit. The second year it made $300,000.

Pat's experience in graphic design began with a part-time job on a local newspaper when she was a freshman in high school, about three years before she wound up at the Community School. One of five sisters and brothers, she grew up on a coastal farm near her grandparents' homestead. "We built forts and went swimming and had gardens and 4-H and all that." She attended the small village grammar school where there were three grades in one room. A quick learner, Pat soon knew the lessons of all three. She made straight A's and loved school.

High school in the more cosmopolitan setting of Ellsworth presented an unsettling transition. Out-of-town kids were looked upon as hicks, and there were problems getting back and forth to participate in after-school activities. Pat found no challenge in the classroom and soon became bored and rebellious. She ran into trouble with authorities when she and a friend started an alternative school paper and published a students' rights handbook. Her group rebelled against the conservative dress code in effect at the school at a time when change in student behavior was sweeping the country. "Things were happening out there that weren't happening in Ellsworth.

"I started skipping school. Skip with other people, go to the Bangor library and sit around, or hitchhike down to the island (Mount Desert) on a nice day, hanging out, drinking a beer, and smoking a joint. I honestly didn't know what I wanted to do. It started in sophomore year and escalated in junior year. At that point it was major, major confrontations at home. I wanted a little bit of leeway, and I couldn't get any. The group of friends I had were all kinds of levels; not bad kids—we just were rebels in a sense. The challenge became seeing how much you could get away with.

"It became really confrontational at home. Then I started running away to Bangor, the island, Massachusetts once. I'd go to school, then go to the bank and get money out of my savings account and take off.

"When I was a freshman, I got a job doing layout and pasteup at a weekly newspaper in Ellsworth. I used to work twenty hours every weekend and after school a couple of days, so that's how I always had money to take off.

"Eventually I went to Connecticut and was gone two weeks. I would call the runaway hot line—I knew all the little things. They'd ask your name and what your pet's name was, and they'd call your parents and ask if they had a dog named so-and-so and say they have a message from your daughter: 'She's fine.'"

The Connecticut trip was the last straw for her parents. Soon after she returned, Pat ended up talking to a probation officer as a habitual runaway. She was directed to a counselor who knew about the Community School just getting started in Camden. She thinks her father drove her to the first interview because the relationship with her mother "was horrible, absolutely horrible. I didn't want to be with her, and she didn't want to be with me."

Pat's first impression of the C-School, then in a small house on Cross Street, remains vivid in her mind after eighteen years. "I thought it was great. There were posters on the walls, and in the front room there were walls of books. I went in and looked, and they were my kind of books—poetry and philosophy. I was excited in that sense. It felt like this was something that I really wanted to do. I knew I couldn't continue to live at home, and it was just going to get worse."

Although the School was struggling to establish itself and gain acceptance in the community, she remembers that it held a real family environment. Students helped with the chores, the shopping, and working in the garden. But for Pat, then only 15, finding a job wasn't easy. She typed for the staff and worked at a day-care center run by a friend of the School. Then she landed a job at a print shop doing graphics and stayed there until she finished school. But the job gave her a degree of independence that figured in her decision to leave the C-School and share an apartment with friends in Camden, two of whom were male.

"I had this job, and I didn't need to go to school anymore. I went home and picked up my belongings. But my mother said no, unbeknownst to me. The police chief came after me and, worst, arrested the two men for aiding and abetting a minor. I went down to the youth center in Hallowell—absolutely the most horrendous thing I ever went through in my life. It was terrifying. I had no idea what was going on. It is absolutely the most sadistic place you have ever been to. The matrons were very much in power situations—dominating, very cold people. There was no counseling, and there were girls in there with problems. I was only there three days in a room with bars. Got locked in your room at night. You had to sleep with your hands outside the covers. Most kids in there can't handle that, so it just escalates."

After three days Pat went to Ellsworth for her court hearing and returned to the Community School as an "emancipated minor." She had to report to a woman probation officer in Rockland once a week. At this point she was so angry at her parents for what they had done, she didn't want to see them.

"There was an environment at the School that nurtured self-thought. There was no 'Memorize this;' it was more an environment of 'Here are the tools; what are you going to do with them?' It was not being shocked at what you told them. I wasn't verbally abused—a relief. I finally had a spot to go where I didn't have to prove anything. It was a time-out place. I didn't have to prove that I was an excellent scholar. I didn't have to prove that I could do a lot of drugs, skip school. I didn't have to prove that I was very good or very bad. I just had to be me.

"I remember one day we went to an island in Muscongus Bay. There was a family feeling. Everything gelled. We were a unit. We had a fire and talked. It was like time stopped that day. Nothing in particular, just the family. I think everybody wants to be in a family. I couldn't be with my family anymore, and I found a new one, and you need that."

Pat finished her term and, along with all the graduates to that time, got her diploma when the School received its accreditation the following February, 1975. She stayed in Camden and with a girl from the School sublet an apartment from someone who neglected to inform the owner of the arrangement. The girls came home one day to find themselves literally on the street.

Pat called her old newspaper in Ellsworth, got a job, and left Camden. She tried living at home but found things "had not changed at all—still a lot of anger." After a month she rented an apartment and moved out. She traveled to Camden often to visit the School, and on one stormy Thanksgiving hitchhiked down with a pumpkin pie—a trip that wound up taking six hours.

When the newspaper folded, she got a job with a small book publisher and lived with a woman farther down east who became a "real catalyst" in her life. About a year later she went to work at the airport near Bar Harbor where she met a pilot. They were married a couple of years later when Pat was 21. By then she had reached a degree of reconciliation with her parents. They wanted to be involved in her wedding, and her father gave her away.

A turning point with her mother came when Pat and her husband moved into the old homestead that had been her grandparents.' Her mother would visit in the evenings, and the two would have long talks. "It patched the pieces, not 100 percent. The whole thing of Hallowell, I get very, very angry. But we do things together; we have great times together."

For seven or eight years after she was married, Pat developed her graphic-arts skills at two key jobs that provided the artistic and business experience that enabled her to open her own shop. When the owner of the last design firm died, customers turned to his partner, Louise Mechaley, and Pat to carry on. The two women took the plunge and started their own company. Even their clients turned out to help them move.

Looking back over the struggle, personal pain, and upheaval that brought her to this point, Pat is reminded of two principles that have guided her since the Community School—the matter of choices and responsibility.

"I had much more freedom there than I did at home, but with that freedom comes a certain responsibility. What you do not only affects yourself but other people—that's the big thing I learned."

"It's OK to make choices, but how do you make those choices? Do you make them rationally, intelligently, with a responsible attitude? 'OK, fine. I'm going to do drugs, and if I do drugs, what's going to happen? I'm only hurting myself.' I could make choices, but how I made them was the key to being responsible. And what has carried through until now is the matter of including others in your choices. How is it going to affect other people—the people I love, the people I work with? That was the key thing."

Now as the mother of a 10-year-old son, she is more acutely aware that making one's own choices is critical to a child's happiness and growth. "We need to teach our children that it is OK to question and allow them to be part of the decisions made about their lives. Some rules—as in the C-School—are unalterable. They must be. But if we allow children full participation in their lives, they stand a better chance of understanding why there are good rules and bad rules. Choices—that was and is the point. When someone makes them for you, it's a hard life if you wake up!"

Although her family life is happy and her business is thriving, Pat is now coping with the aftermath of the most irrevocable course change of her life—the devastating fire that recently destroyed her home and everything she and her family possessed. She writes about it poignantly and with a courageous strength of spirit: "Lost in the ashes are years of journals and artwork, letters and photos that were my personal history, poetry written in the deep pits of despair and the soaring heights of joy, faces of friends looking out from glossy prints, letters from my grandmother, lovers, and friends. It is frustrating to have lost that center on reality, what was real, what is mist. In my mind's eye I try to recreate. I am successful at times; yet too often I still mourn. Beginnings are tough, but endings are harder, so I am trying to make a new beginning. The slate doesn't like being clean.

"What is most real from this loss is that I understand that while these items were important to my life, I still have me. Many dreams were shattered with that fire, many plans undone, but an opportunity exists to restructure without baggage. And is that not the true essence of life—to take what you are given and mold it into something that makes you happy?"

Suzanne Bowden

"The interview? It was real quiet. I think Dora and Emanuel were still learning a lot, and I remember my mother doing most of the talking. There weren't a lot of questions, and it didn't take very long either. I think they were still learning what rules to put in and what to ask and stuff."

That's how Suzanne Bowden recalls her interview in 1974 with Dora Lievow and Emanuel Pariser, Co-directors of the fledgling Community School they had started in Camden scarcely a year before.

Suzanne was 17 and had dropped out of school in West Springfield, Massachusetts. For the better part of two years, she and a group of friends had been skipping school, hanging out, and getting high. "I thought the school system was strange—thirty to forty kids in a classroom. If you never showed up, they never noticed anyway. I had no academic problem. I could do it if I tried. I just didn't try."

There were six kids in Suzanne's family, only one of whom made it through high school. Her father, a truck driver, was away from home for long periods while her mother stayed home and took care of the house and family. Sometimes Suzanne lived away from home, usually with a woman whose daughter could do anything she wanted. "I could stay there all the time. I worked, but any money I got went right straight for drugs—not into any of the real drugs that people were screwing up with—alcohol was probably the biggest. Quite a few of us would drink a lot."

When Suzanne had her C-School interview, she was in Camden on her annual summer visit with her grandmother and already had said she wanted to stay the winter. Her mother had seen an article about the new school in the local newspaper, and both she and Suzanne's grandmother urged her to apply.

Suzanne waited a month before hearing that she had been accepted for the coming fall term, 1974. With four other students and the Co-directors, the small house on Cross Street where the School began all but bulged at the seams. "It was close quarters. It got to the point that Phil (a student) and I realized we could share a room better than anybody because the rest wanted to kill each other in the same bedroom.

"There weren't too many rules. When I was there, Phil made homemade beer, and Dora and Emanuel were going away every other weekend and had this other man come in to watch over us. But I think they got in their mind that they had to settle back and make more rules. They learned a lot with each class."

Suzanne had few problems with the academics and was surprised that she "actually did" algebra. She got a good job for the term with a Maine winterization project, the first woman on such a crew in the state. She had a great time on the job which often entailed working out of town for a day or two. After she graduated, she stayed with the job for the final six months of the state contract.

"I learned a lot about living with other people at the School. In our family we just kept quiet and went our separate ways. When you live in a house like that where nobody kept quiet, you kind of had to get along with each other. Sometimes we didn't, and sometimes we did. It's not so bad now, but back then I had a real bitchy side to me and used to get ruffled now and then. But I think my own kids took it out of me. It's kind of hard to get real mad at a little kid when those big eyes look at you."

Suzanne graduated in March of 1975 and did not return to West Springfield. She got a job at a precision instrument manufacturing firm in Camden and worked there five years. The delicate tool work, done under a magnifying glass, is performed largely by women. "I didn't like the work as much as I liked the women. When you get a lot of women working together, it can be fun, and it can be funny."

She was married in 1980 to an officer in the merchant marine. They lived for about four years in New Hampshire when their two boys, Nicholas and Nathanial, were toddlers. But she felt too isolated with her husband's three-months-at-sea and three-months-at-home schedule, and they moved back to Camden. They bought a candle and gift business which Suzanne managed successfully for several years. Although she lives nearby, Suzanne seldom contacts the School and has never been in the larger house it has occupied since the late seventies.

"There were times during the term when I said, 'I really don't want to finish this,' but then there was no place to go. I knew my grandmother wouldn't want me there; she wanted me to finish school. I don't think I really knew at the time whether I wanted to finish. I don't think I really cared. The first few months were really rotten at times. After that I had so much done I thought I might as well finish. But I hate to think what would have happened if I'd stayed in Springfield and kept on going like I was."

Angie Eagan Wildhaber

By the time she was 21, Angie Eagan had worked a skidder in the Maine woods, homesteaded in Alaska bear territory, and played too fast for her own good with hard-core bikers. Like way stations on a highway, these sojourns linked the frenzied five years she hitched back and forth across the country and into Mexico.

She was barely 16 when she left home with nothing more than a pack on her back. "Truck drivers would pick me up, and I learned to deal with them—talk fast, you know—and it worked. I got my act straightened out a little bit from there." She often slept in the woods and "spent a lot of time getting eaten up by mosquitoes." When her pack was stolen, a man she met in a restaurant gave her some blankets and jeans. In another state a young guy took her home to his mother for the night because he didn't want to see her "out on the street." She would stop a month or so in some towns and get a job waitressing to earn money before hitting the road again.

"I've always been adventuresome," she says, happily innocent of the understatement. Yet as you listen to this 33-year-old woman, her face beaming as she sits hugging her little daughter, her story strains belief. Full-bodied with a tumble of tawny hair, she appears settled far beyond the life she led a short time ago. Angie alternately laughs and talks in a torrent of words, verbally leaping forward and back over those years as kinetically as she once shuttled across the country.

"We lived in Kenai. There were brown bear not far from the house. We squatted off some land, found an abandoned camp, stripped it, and piped water in. After about one year living there, I bought some land. We threw a party—had a keg of beer and homemade food—and all of us built a log cabin home in a day. Throughout the week we put in doors and windows. Before we got a generator, we used an alternator from a car—hooked it up to a snowmobile and charged a 12-volt battery. We had lights, TV, and music. We lived there three years."

Angie went to Alaska by ferryboat on her honeymoon with her first husband whom she met on the West Coast. "We didn't know much when we got there. We had to work with what was there at the time. I learned a lot from the camping and mountain-climbing trips the Community School took us on every month. The things I learned from Dora and Emanuel helped us out a lot."

Angie had been out of the C-School long enough to get into trouble with some bike gangs in Rockland which precipitated her cross-country travels. She was dating a biker and soon was running and drinking with members of several gangs—the Ironhorsemen, NSKK, and Hell's Angels.

"We would just go ride Harley Davidsons. I thought it was cool—the smell of the leather and the sounds of the bikes and the feeling of being free from it all on a bike. I was 16, young, and naive. The bikers were the ones who rooted out the helmet law, and after that we pretty much took over Rockland. I realized everything was getting too rowdy and out of control. I couldn't go into a bar or out dancing without getting into a fight and having to leave the bar.

"I woke up one day and realized I really didn't want to live that way. But I had so much energy that I couldn't go from what I was doing to a living-at-home, folding-napkins type of deal. So I just took off out of town and started hitchhiking across the country."

Angie's troubles at home took root when she arrived in Rockland at age 8 from Munich, Germany, to live with her father's people. Angie could speak no English, and no one could understand her. She had to repeat kindergarten, and as her father was in the US Army, she changed schools many times throughout the country. Her German-born mother, sister, and brother remained in Germany out of contact for some years. For a time when she very young, Angie thought her mother was coming to take her and another sister back to Germany, but she never came.

"I guess I was rebelling because my mother never came back and my Dad was dying. I was a smart aleck in school. The teachers couldn't handle me. I was more interested in the older guys and girls. They were having more fun." In her first year in the Lisbon High School in her stepmother's hometown, Angie's counselor gave her two choices: an inland farm school or the Community School.

"I really liked the Community School. The teachers were like none I ever saw before. They never gave me ultimatums. They'd say, 'We're not going to deal with you if you are going to be smoking pot or coming in drunk. You choose.' They were forever giving us choices. I learned that you've got to take responsibility. I learned a lot even from kids at the School because it brought the picture out a lot clearer: 'Hey, this is what you're doing too,' and I didn't like it. But it took me seeing it in the other kids to make me realize I gotta change my ways."

Customary School activities delighted Angie. She recalls spinning a wheel on the wall to decide who did what household chore and writing thoughts she might not express verbally in the student log book. "We would say, 'I didn't realize that's how you felt.' It helped us because we were a group of kids who didn't know how to get our feelings out."

Angie was a student during the Community School's earliest years. "I remember Emanuel telling me that they were the learning ones. They made their mistakes along with our mistakes, and we grew from each other. Since we broke almost every rule there was, they've changed a lot of them now. They have a lot of patience with younger kids. I don't think I would be able to do it because they take boys and girls that have had a lot of problems—head troubles or emotional troubles—and I don't ever remember them losing it on us."

Angie left the School before she finished her term and went to work on a farm nearby with one hundred head of cattle to feed. This is where she worked in the woods and learned to operate a skidder. "But I really wanted to get my education. Dora and Emanuel were still patient with me and welcomed me back when I wanted to do it." Angie didn't live at the School this time but took her academic classes at the YMCA and met with a counselor once a week. One snowy night during the School's winter term, she graduated with the current class.

"I've always kept in touch with them since I was 16 years old. I'd write a letter or call them up. If I needed a reference, Emanuel would have it right out to me. Or they'd send me the newspaper even when I went to Alaska."

When she returned from Alaska, Angie divorced her husband and worked in California waitressing or doing jobs with "mud, tape, and texture" (sheetrockers' lingo). During this time she met the man who became her daughter Renee's father. "We never married. He was a dreamer, a drifter. After Renee was born, I had to seek a lot of assistance because her dad took off. He couldn't handle the pressure because he was five years younger than I was. I pretty much raised her myself."

Angie returned to Rockland with Renee after her father died. She has other family members there, but she finds that the love and closeness she felt from her father "could never be replaced." She has not seen her sister in Germany for eighteen years, but she has been reunited with her other sister and mother.

Angie is now married to Chris Wildhaber, a Californian whom she met in Reno. "He may be ten years younger, but he is helping to raise Renee. He loves her and says, 'She's my little girl.' We joke about it now—about the way I used to live and the way I am now—because now I haven't done anything exciting."

Bob Enman

Bob Enman was pretty much on his own from his 14th year as far as doing what he wanted to do. He got odd jobs on his neighbor's chicken farm, with a mechanic who assembled electric motors, and in the woods on the family property where his father ran a logging business.

Bob grew up in a rural area outside of town, the middle one of five boys. He had started elementary school in North Carolina which has a later age requirement, so in Brunswick he was a year or more older than most of the kids in his class. He got through elementary school with no problems; however, junior high was a different story; school was no longer one of his priorities. He often missed the bus on purpose, so he'd have to hitch a ride to school in Brunswick. Then he'd decide not to go after all.

"I started getting real wild into drugs and alcohol. I was a long-haired hippie then—late sixties, early seventies. The friends I had did that sort of thing. I didn't get A's anymore. I passed without even trying. In math class the teacher didn't care if I showed up just so I came in Fridays and passed the test in general math. I took all easy classes that I could breeze through and not have to study."

The school guidance counselor asked Bob if he'd like to go to a counseling group in Brunswick called Full Circle that was setting up weekly sessions for school kids. "We could go in and talk, smoke cigarettes, sit around, and do nothing. Sounded fine to me."

As it turned out, the man who ran Full Circle became a staunch friend and a major influence in his life. Bob remembers being so eager to go to these sessions that he arrived early once and broke in. "I'd do stuff like that, just break into something, a car, to see if I could do it. In summer we went on camping trips. I didn't kick booze or drugs, but we'd talk. I couldn't talk to anybody at home. My family wasn't like that, couldn't sit down and talk about problems."

The Full Circle leader was taking a member of the group to the Community School for an interview and asked Bob if he'd like to go along. He did and unexpectedly got an interview right after the other boy. He doesn't remember much about it. "The only thing in my head was, 'In six months I can have my diploma, and I won't have to go to school until I'm 20 years old.'"

About a week later his Full Circle leader told him he was accepted for the term already in progress. Bob was 17 and had not officially dropped out of his sophomore year in high school. He also had to break the news to his parents who did not want him to go. "But I said, 'In five months I'm going to be 18, and I'm going to quit.' So they reluctantly let me go, took me up there, dropped me off, and left."

The young school was in its second and somewhat larger home in Camden, and Bob remembers that his class led the staff a merry chase. He had no problem with the academics and enjoyed the job he had at a day-care center in Rockland. He had trouble with the physical-contact rule on one occasion and got suspended for two weeks when he climbed out on the school roof and smoked marijuana. A student from the previous term spotted him and turned him in. He had a close call with the law when he was arrested in Rockland for possession of marijuana. "It wasn't mine; it was a friend's. He was starting some trouble, and I took it away from him so he wouldn't get caught with it. They grabbed him, and I said something, and they grabbed me.

"Dora and Emanuel came down, and they talked to them (the police). I thought I was done. I thought I was going to be out. The police were going to kick me out of Rockland. But I said I worked there, and they said, "OK, but then stay out of town." So I didn't go to jail and didn't get kicked out of school. I had two people who really cared about kids, and I hadn't seen that before except for Jeff Smith (the Full Circle counselor). And I was smart enough to know what I needed to do to get through the course."

That knowledge wasn't enough to stop Bob from playing the stereotypical 17-year-old to the hilt. With great festivity he threw an 18th birthday party for himself at a favorite class hangout a couple of months ahead of schedule so he could legally buy drinks there. Emanuel had planned to begin a psychology class that night. "We watched him from the lounge—the windows were right on the street—and he came in and asked if we were going to come to class. We said no. He turned around and left, and we never had another psychology class. Our group was probably the biggest for doing things as a team. Whether it was good or bad, we did it together. They have a lot more rules now than they did then."

From his present vantage point as a father with school-age kids, Bob views some of his C-School pranks more "teenage stuff" compared to the hard drugs he was doing in Brunswick. At the same time he recognizes how sorely his group's thoughtless behavior must have tried staff souls.

"We did some mean things to Emanuel. He did a trust thing where he got up on a table and fell backwards, and nobody caught him. He hadn't forgotten that the last time I talked to him. It still bothers him that nobody would catch him. All it was to us was a joke. I think he did it at the wrong time, right at the beginning of the term. Trust wasn't a big thing. At that point we didn't know anybody."

When graduation came, Bob had stayed with his job, paid his bills, and was the only one in his class to get a diploma. Soon after, he went into the service for a couple of years, got married, and gave up drugs. He supports a growing family and for a time considered starting a school similar to the C-School.

"If it was not for the Community School, I would have quit at 18 and probably gotten a diploma somewhere. But more than that, it was a family. I had four brothers and a mother and a father, but it wasn't a family. I'd do it again."

Heidi Tibbetts

Heidi Tibbetts lives a stone's throw from Passamaquoddy Bay in Eastport. Through the house plants that crowd her windows, she can look across to Deer Island, New Brunswick. Hers is one of the older houses in the town— a roomy, rambling structure comfortably shared at any hour by the three children in her family, their friends, cousins, and family dogs. It has taken almost 15 years, two disappointing marriages, and some lean, lonely times, but Heidi, at last, has a stable, happy family of her own.

Heidi was the youngest in her family, and because of a difference in ages she grew up as an only child—in her words, "rotten spoiled." Her mother, strict and protective in some matters, was quite permissive about Heidi's schooling. "If I decided I didn't want to go to school, I just didn't go. And there was never any question about it at home." The pattern continued on into high school where, because of her spotty attendance, she started failing. At this time she became increasingly disturbed by problems at home, particularly when an older sister with two small children came home to live. Suddenly Heidi lost her place as the youngest and only child.

"Everything in those two years was real chaotic. We were all living in a real small trailer in Eastport, and I just wanted to get away from it. I was 16 and had stopped going to school almost entirely. I didn't drink or hang out; I was a loner, sociable but a loner. I knew I could handle things alone. Of course I didn't know what handling things meant at that point."

Heidi found her home situation so upsetting that she developed stomach problems for which her doctor prescribed tranquilizers. He also suggested she see a counselor in Machias. There Heidi heard about the Community School and was interested enough to apply. Her sister drove her to Camden for the interview. The School's 1975 fall term was just starting. Heidi liked the place immediately, but her sister was not impressed and fought against the idea when they got home.

Heidi had learned early how to deal with such situations. "When I asked my mother if I wanted to do anything, no matter how reasonable it was, the answer was no. So I learned to stop asking and just say, 'I'm going to do this,' and nobody ever questioned it. So I said, 'I like the place, and I'm going to do it,' and nobody questioned it."

At that time the School took six students per term, and Heidi was the fourth. Adjusting to the other kids was difficult at first. One used drugs, and the other two had come from juvenile detention homes. "It was a culture shock. The first couple of weeks were a matter of getting used to a different way of life."

Heidi had no problem with her studies and passed her tests with good scores. She got a job soon after she arrived as a teacher's aide working with retarded children. But she did not share the enthusiasm for camping trips held by the majority of students who have attended the Community School. Difficult as it may be to understand, a camping trip prevented her from getting her diploma.

"I hated camping trips with a bloody passion. The second trip I freaked out so thoroughly that we never even made it to the top of that mountain. I remember bursting into tears and being so tired and so wiped out that I couldn't cope with it—the heights, the activity, the cold. I'm just not an outdoors person.

"I was succeeding at the School. I was graduating. I was seeing something through the whole way, but I didn't make it through. I had my moment of rebellion, quit, and went home just four weeks shy of graduation."

Heidi had completed all the tests for her GED but did not receive her Community School diploma because the camping trip was a requirement. She called soon after she got home and asked to return to the School. But in addition to the camping trip, she was told that one of her requirements was "to stay out Saturday night until curfew. Mind you, I would much rather curl up with a book while everybody else was out partying." Still she missed the School and went back to visit as often as she could for a while. She seriously considered going back to complete her diploma requirements when she learned through the Outreach/Aftercare Program that an environmental activity could satisfy the camping credit. A personal tragedy temporarily shelved that plan which she wants to pursue at a later date.

Heidi stayed at home in Eastport for a short time after she left the Community School and enrolled in the University of Maine at Machias. Later that year she got married. She was 17, and he was 20. The marriage lasted five years during which Heidi had a boy and a girl as well as several miscarriages. After the divorce she lived alone with her children in a trailer that belonged to her parents and got along on AFDC assistance. She got several jobs, but with the cost of day care she lost money working. A few years later she married again and had another daughter, but it didn't work out. Now happily settled with a mature partner, Heidi manages home and family and juggles several part-time jobs.

"It's the second time in my life that I've had a family—here with John and all the children and before at the Community School. I don't think any of us who were there that term thought of it as a school. It was a family. I don't think I'm unique about that. A lot of us had our differences, but when push came to shove, we were a family. It still seems like my extended family.

"At the School I learned to accept myself, that I was OK, that I could say, 'This is the way I do things. You don't have to meet my expectations, and I won't meet yours.' I had responsibilities, but I didn't have to prove myself, just do the best I could. I grew up there. I went from being a super-dependent child to being responsible for myself. I learned how to deal with people in a more constructive way."

Tony Duveau

Tony Duveau came home from school one day and walked into a big family fight. His mother, sisters, and brothers were splitting up. Home, however unstable, was disintegrating before his very eyes. The question uppermost in the division of family spoils was, "Who's going to take Tony?" Bewildered, Tony, the next youngest of six siblings, found himself not only a victim but part of the problem. "I'll take Cindy but not Tony" tolls in his memory today. Now in his early thirties, he watches his three young sons playing on the living room floor and vows, "I don't care what I have to do; they're not going to go through what I went through."

Although he is happily married, comfortably settled in a low-mortgage ranch-style house, and nearing the end of his truck-driver's training course, he finds it hard to shed the resentment and bitterness he harbors for his young life. "No one ever showed me anything in my life, you know. I mean, 'Just get out of here and play.' All my mother wanted was a Social Security check, so she didn't care what I did."

Tony was 17 and just entering high school at the time the family broke up. Performance in school reflected the indifference with which it was held at home. "My mother was there, but she wasn't. There wasn't any supervision. There was a party every weekend at the house. Actually, I was pretty wild."

He went to live with an older sister who had an apartment—a period he sums up in two words, "oh, god," with a groan and roll of his eyes.

Tony continued to attend the local high school where he recalls he was absent only three days but got twenty-one detentions. "I got put down for all kinds of stuff—drinking, everything else. I hardly ever drank anyway. One day I skipped school to work because I was short of cash. I only got arrested twice in my life and once was for speeding. Basically it got to the point of arguing in the family: 'What are we going to do with Tony? He's 17 years old. Let's just send him somewhere.' Great family. They thought of a place in Portland, but I wasn't that messed up."

His sister heard about the Community School from the local Community Action Center and called for information. "She wanted to get rid of me herself" was Tony's reaction. But he went to the School for what he remembers as an "intensive" interview. "It helped me realize myself what I had in my own head and what I wanted to do. I think that's what made the interview good and brought me into the School in the first place."

Tony entered the fall term, 1977, but failed to get his diploma in the spring—"just plain neglect. I didn't finish a few things; didn't pay attention enough." The program proved more demanding than anything he had faced before. Not least was the everyday challenge of learning to be responsible for himself, getting a job, and meeting his household obligations. "I never had to do anything like that. I never had the responsibility of having to earn money, pay rent, and cover everything to feed myself. I had no concept of what life was really like. Finding a job there was tough, and employers didn't make it easy for you." He worked at two jobs during the term and is proud that he had paid his rent in full by graduation.

Academics were difficult for Tony, not only because of a learning problem and poor preparation but, as he says, "I was the kind of kid that figured 'What the hell? Do I got to know the exact date Columbus came over and touched land with his boat?" Still, he appreciated the practical skills that are basic to the Community School program. "They were teaching you something you had to know if all else failed—to take care of yourself and live on your own and keep a roof over your head. Even filling out an application: Fill out every little spot; they look for neatness. And they helped me get a job."

Family problems continued to plague Tony during the term. He remembers as his worst experience there the time his mother and her boyfriend arrived and tried to enter the School to forcibly take him away. Even the mention of the School's camping trips, which he enjoyed, brings to mind a family camping trip his mother arranged. "She dropped us kids off at the campsite, then said 'good-bye,' and took off with her boyfriend. Nice family get-together. That camping trip with the C-School was more like a family than my own."

Education, the first step out of poverty, does not come readily to hand for the disadvantaged. Tony left the C-School with his rent paid but his work unfinished. He went back to his hometown and got a job washing dishes in a restaurant. That's where he met Molly, and they started going together. But inside he was restless. He realized he had to go back to school. "I felt I needed something to fall back on. I hitchhiked up there, got an apartment, got a job, and went to school." This time he went to the C-School only for classes and otherwise lived completely independent of School supervision. When he was laid off his job, he found another as a public-school janitor under the CETA program. Tony was putting into practice the life skills he had absorbed during his initial term at the Community School.

It took many months and a good measure of hard work and persistence on Tony's part, but he finally got his diploma. He had hitchhiked back to see Molly every weekend throughout this period; now that he had graduated and finished his work, he felt there was nothing left for him in the area. Molly became pregnant, and in a couple of months they were married but not without some family intervention.

"We weren't going to get married, just keep it the way it was," Molly says. "But with an old Italian family it was more like, 'If you're going to stay together and going to have a baby, you might as well, you know." Tony wanted to wait until the baby was born and "crawling around a little bit" so they could take a honeymoon. Instead, they got married and moved to Queens, New York, where Molly's family hailed from. "I guess that was my worst mistake," says Tony. "We should have stayed in Maine right where we were. Things would have gone a lot smoother."

Tony worked at a variety of plumbing and security jobs, but living expenses were high. No matter how much he worked—two jobs most of the time—things got progressively worse financially. He and Molly held out for three years. By that time they had their second boy. "One day I just got mad. Molly paid the rent and had absolutely nothing left, so we packed it up and came back to Maine." They went first to his mother's. "We were supposed to stay until we found a place, but we stayed one night. My mother got in a fight with Molly and threw her and the kids out, but it was 'OK for Tony to stay.' I was so angry."

The next several years taxed every survival skill he and Molly possessed. No sooner had they found a place to stay than Molly was hospitalized in

Portland with a difficult pregnancy that resulted in the premature birth of their third son, Joey. That necessitated their move to Portland to be near the hospital. "We moved up here basically because Joey was only 1 pound 14 ounces when he was born. Been here ever since because of the care unit they have up here." Right after the baby was born, Tony lost his job. The ensuing months brought a seemingly constant scramble for work coupled with two or three apartment moves and concern over Joey's fragile condition as well as the care of their two preschool youngsters.

"Finally we got lucky. A friend of Molly's was having a bad time, so we just took over her payments and got this house." It is located in a rural community outside of Portland, and the boys can go to school right up the street. "They're making all A's and B's. My kids are a pleasure." Molly is associated with Head Start and is a center director.

Their daily work schedule hinges on split-second connections. In order to take his truck-driving course, Tony commutes to New Hampshire—a two-hour drive—every day for classes that run from 6 p.m. to 5 a.m. As soon as class is over, he drives back to Maine, arriving home by 7 so Molly can leave for work at 7:15.

Reflecting on the years since he felt lost and unwanted as a teenager, Tony points to the simple realities of life: "The reality of living on your own—collect your rent receipts, pay your electric bill, take care of the oil man, handle your money, your responsibilities in general—that's a big thing. A lot of people don't know that.

"You pick up your pieces, correct your mistakes. A person that makes a mistake can't expect someone else to pick up the pieces and solve the problem that they created themselves. If you can't fix your own problem, you might as well hang it up on life. Like my boys—if I can't fix my own problems, how can I help them with theirs?"

As he looks ahead, it is obvious Tony has gained the self-confidence he lacked as a youth. "My five-year plan is to be the owner/operator of my own tractor trailer and within that time go to school for diesel mechanics. That way if I get stuck on the side of the road, all I got to do is pull out my tool box."

Brenda and George Elliott

"I hated the school system, hated competitive sports, hated phys ed. Home life was turmoil with five kids in the family, and nothing I ever did was good enough. I ran away off and on, quit school, got on probation." Brenda Elliott, copper-haired and freckled, never has had any trouble expressing herself. Her laugh bubbles along as she pours out an image of her teenage self growing up in Calais on the Canadian border in the mid-seventies. "I told my probation officer, 'I just can't live at home. We're going to rip each other apart. Either you find an alternative, or I'm going to run.'"

Her husband, George, sitting beside her on their living-room couch, can scarcely contain his grin. A soft-voiced man of few words, he reacts less explosively to trying situations. When he didn't feel he was learning much after two years at Camden High School back in the seventies, he dropped out and went to work in the sardine plant in Rockland. "I was into partying and couldn't see myself going to night school, and I sure didn't see going back to high school." He partied sometimes with the kids at the Community School, just around the corner from his house. That's where he met Brenda in the spring term of 1977.

Brenda liked the sound of the School from the moment she read the brochure her probation officer gave her. She felt even better about the interview, and as a student loved the whole term. "They treated me like I had an opinion, like a real human being. It was wonderful from day one."

She and George started going together soon after they met, and during her term she persuaded him to apply. He was accepted and entered that fall, right after her class graduated. While George attended school, Brenda lived at his mother's house, now their home. The following year they became the first graduates to get married— barely four years after the School began. They now have two boys, Uriah 7 and Logan 3.

While Brenda found the School gave her "more freedom than my own parents had ever given me," George chafed under the loss of freedom to drive his car. Reticent by nature, he had a difficult time at the weekly Group Rap. "There was a lot of stress in it. I didn't have anything to complain about." Brenda interjects, "They wanted feelings. They wanted to know what was going on with George." But George, speaking for himself then and now, says simply, "I'm not very good about expressing myself."

While she was a student, Brenda developed a family possessiveness about the School that has diminished only slightly over the years. She remembers getting in trouble for coming back late from a trip. After that she made an effort to get everybody back on time. "I was kind of a worry wart, I suppose. I worried about the School and what people would say if they saw us out after curfew because it was during that whole mess with the town hating the School and not wanting it there. I felt that we as students had to prove the town wrong. I took that on as a personal battle. It really was. We were the first term to have to go up against this kind of hatred, and we had to prove them wrong." Two years earlier the School had appealed a Planning Board decision denying them permission to relocate to a larger building. Despite heated protests from some quarters of the community, the appeal was granted.

George went back to the sardine plant right after he graduated and worked there eight years. He left to take a responsible job at an internationally known seaweed products firm in Rockland where he has been ever since. Brenda also worked at the sardine plant for a few years but has devoted her time to parenting since the boys were born. In recent years she has worked for a local farmer harvesting beans, haying, and helping out with the sheep at lambing and shearing time. "I like it. It gets me out of the house, and I always wanted to be on a farm anyway."

Brenda felt a sense of loss for some time after she graduated from the C-School. "I wanted to go back. I was homesick. I saw other people taking my place that I had so treasured. There was a part of me that was jealous, and yet I felt good that they were getting what I had gotten out of it."

Reflecting on the School's impact on her personal development, Brenda recalls her rage as a teenager. "I was so angry—angry with my parents, angry with that whole age group, the whole philosophy of how they thought kids should be treated. I was bitter. I had no trust, no faith; didn't want anything to do with any of them. I met people through the C-School in every age group who thought the same way I did, even people my parents' age. That was the first time I had ever really seen that. I needed to see that there were people who had the same type of philosophy and that I wasn't abnormal. I had thought something was wrong with me because I couldn't conform to my parents and what they believed. Their beliefs were so different from mine and are still. But they have seen how my children are turning out, and I think that's made a difference in my relationship with them."

Brenda also recognizes a growing maturity in herself, particularly in relation to her parents. "It's one of understanding, forgiveness, tolerance. And I've gotten that through my own children."

Although she lives right around the corner, Brenda has lost some of her sense of contact with the Community School. "It's been hard at times. Sometimes I think they see me as one of their statistics, and I see them as family." She touches on the communal closeness that many students in the School's early years say they felt toward the staff and each other. "The fact that they weren't that much older somehow made it easier for us to trust them. But I think they are beginning to fit that parental age group more than they did then. They're wrapped up in their own lives. The kids there now don't feel like they're a whole family unit like it used to be."

She and George agree that the School was a big plus at a very crucial period for each of them. "You are so torn at that time of life. Part of you wants to be a kid, and part of you is demanding to be treated as an adult, and you're just halfway in between."

David Buffinton

As a youngster growing up in Rockport, David Buffinton gave early promise of topping out at his present 6 feet 6 inches. Lanky, open-faced, and quietly curious, David steered a more divergent course than those of his older brother and sister. Like them, he had gone to private schools and camps and learned to handle boats at the family's summer place on one of Maine's islands. But when it came to school, David's interests lay elsewhere. He was 15 and in his sophomore year at Camden-Rockport High School when he dropped out.

About that time he was walking up the street with a friend who spotted a parked car with the keys in the ignition. His friend suggested going for a ride, and David jumped in. They picked up another friend, then left the car, and eventually faced the police. The boys' reprimand involved a stint of community service. A short time later David went out of state to live with his father and was enrolled in a private school late in its term.

"It didn't work out. I was pretty much rebelling." Back home in Rockport his mother suggested the Community School. David applied and was accepted for the following term, spring of 1977. "The thing I liked was the one-to-one tutoring. In high school if I still didn't understand after I'd asked a question, I didn't feel like raising my hand again, so I just let it go over my head." By contrast, at the C-School "You're studying material you're going to take the test on. So if it's not clear, you can talk to your tutor about it. Averaging all my scores, I had the highest to date of the C-School. That impressed me. But then someone next term broke my record."

Aside from academics David started out a bit rebellious at the Community School and wound up overstepping bounds on his job that could have involved serious trouble. Handy around boats, he was a natural for his School job pumping out the bilge of a power boat in the harbor. He pumped the bilge one day and on the spur of the moment took the boat for a lengthy spin around the nearby islands and burned up a lot of fuel on the ride.

"Luckily, I didn't damage anything. The owner was out of town and that's why I regretted taking advantage of the situation. Took a couple of friends, probably had a couple of beers, and went over to Rockport, then Islesboro, then back to Camden. I was supposed to cook dinner that night, and I was late. That was the last crazy thing I did at the C-School. There was a discussion at Group Rap that week, and the responsibility started to set in. I wanted to get a diploma to please my family for one thing."

But partying was still big in his life as it was for others in his term. On the School's annual weekend in Boston, David, a former resident, felt he could breeze the class through the "treasure hunt"—a mapped course to pick up a brochure or sticker from various city landmarks—"so we could get a beer or a smoke or something. But they dropped us off at MIT, and I didn't know where the heck we were. Wandered for blocks before we found a subway."

During the School term David also worked for a carpenter and a chowder house and baked bread at a gourmet restaurant—sixty loaves each morning. He graduated in the fall of 1977 and shared a tiny top-floor room at the restaurant with a classmate for a couple of months. "I felt a little more responsible after graduation—no more stealing cars or boats." But partying, drinking, smoking pot, and showing up late for work continued.

He moved to Portland a few months later and got an apartment and a job with a glass company where he has been employed for 12 years. He met Sharon, a level-headed, earthy young woman, over a cribbage game at a bar. They soon moved into a small apartment together—a relationship that was a turning point in David's life. Partying began to lose its former priority. He and Sharon now have lived nine years in the house they bought in Gray. David has built most of their furniture, combining glass and wood. They put their creative talents together and won two consecutive awards in the annual Kennebec River Whatever Race—a popular state event featuring imaginatively festooned watercraft.

Although he's seldom in touch with the School, he says, "That may have been the only way I would have gotten a diploma was going to a school like that."

Settling In

1978 - 1985

After ten terms we recognized patterns of student behavior: The first two to four weeks were often a honeymoon period; the School was such a welcome change from previous situations that everything felt new and wonderful. A second stage emerged when old behaviors and attitudes asserted themselves creating conflict in the community. One staff member wrote in the staff log, circa 1981, "So that's what's in the air: missing money, mystery relationships, sexual harassment on the job, a student just left, another one coming....(We have the) feeling that it's rare when the students are honest."

Crises occured every forty days of the 160-day term. Students decided to leave or recommit to the program at these times, and we held our breath as their choices were made. The excitement and energy generated by a choice to stay often injected a positive, directed feeling into the continuing students. But at term's end their behavior and attitude often returned to the old, familiar, and unproductive ways of coping as if in preparation for reentering the real world.

The "me" decade brought a modicum of prosperity to Maine, and the early eighties were almost bustling with economic activity as real estate markets expanded. Jobs for students were easier to find, and federal CETA programs, not immediately gutted by the Reagan era, offered job training.

Despite these signs of economic health some of the School's state funds were imperiled by budget cuts, and we launched our first letter-writing, lobbying campaign to the state legislature. Although small, our program had reached students throughout Maine, enabling us to tap several legislators on our behalf. In the summer of 1979 our $15,000 State Corrections grant was restored.

In 1978 Dora and I married, and in 1980 we had our first child. The novelty of having a young child around the School wore off quickly, especially for staff who had no children of their own. No longer could we both attend all School activities, breaking the tradition that everyone did certain elements of the program such as camping trips, Group Rap, and the first day of school. Dora scaled back her hours but kept essentially the same responsibilities. Resentments surfaced when expectations were established for the co-directors different from those for other staff. Faculty questioned whether the School was straying from its original structure as a non-hierarchical, consensus-based organization.

The arrival of our second son in 1983 increased the necessity to redefine staff roles and expectations. Our faculty at this time tended to be in their late twenties, single or in relationships, and without other primary responsibilities. With two exceptions, the School has never been able to employ live-in teacher/counselors with children of their own for more than a year. Staff schedules averaging 50 to 60 hours per week in 1980 slowly diminished to the current 44 hours per week by 1985. At the same time the sense of tight-knit collegiality and undifferentiated staff structure seemed to fade. In some respects the job began to be "normal," although all staff made extraordinary financial sacrifices to work at the School, the average pay being around $7 per hour.

To keep us from dwelling too much on internal changes that were rapidly altering our staff culture, the external world posed a new threat. Influenced by the Nation-at-Risk movement, Maine Legislators enacted the Education Reform Act of 1984 which, among other things, increased graduation requirements for all students.

The Department of Education began to reconsider the Community School's unorthodox, although previously approved, methods of granting diplomas. Those in charge of school approval raised the issues of seat time, number of days in the school year, and how these translated into the carnegie units necessary for graduation. With luck, good timing, and the intervention of one well-placed lawyer, the movement to strip the School of its diploma-granting capacity was stalled. The Department did not want a legal or legislative fight on its hands over a tiny school which dealt with students whom some considered marginal at best.

Although mentioned in the Reform Act, alternative schools and programs for dropouts were not of central concern. Our nation was "at risk" because we weren't sufficiently competitive with Japan; "raising standards" was seen as the way to win the economic battle. (I have yet to meet a student or teacher who is inspired by this argument to learn or teach.)

By 1984 one staff member had worked with us five years, and several others made extended commitments to the program. The School had lost its original consultant, worked with two new ones, and weathered a six-month leave-of-absence by Dora and myself.

Over these six years America's consciousness of substance abuse, violence, sexuality, and gender issues rose dramatically. Resources were beginning to be available to help our students plagued with drug and alcohol issues; counseling, AA, and treatment were all highly beneficial on occasion.

Through the work of staff member Bob Dickens, effective tutorials and seminars were held on violence, substance abuse, and parenting. The School continued to conceptualize its mission as primarily educational rather than therapeutic.

A staff member wrote in 1982, "Caving was a lot of fun. I found myself slightly irritated with how macho J and P are but also with how frail and helpless E and S acted to foster this." We wrestled with such issues. How accepting or rejecting were we to be of the traditional macho male role and the reciprocally passive and unassertive female role which many of our students played out? Where could we begin with the volatile issue of homophobia? How much change could we expect in 160 days?

Throughout hours of dialog the School managed the tension between the political and the personal. We weighed the often conflicting needs of staff and students and tried to treat each situation on its own merits rather than on precedent or dogma. We were not always successful.

Much changed and much stayed the same. Personal encounters between staff and students infused the program with treasured moments of incidental learning. As I recorded in my log, "I talked with J about life-styles over a mop. After I had succinctly put my philosophy of life into two paragraphs, she pointed out the spot on the floor I had missed with my mop."

More students finished their terms, and the program continued to gain credibility in the community. For the first time we reaccepted one of our our own dropouts; we began adapting some of our original beliefs. —EP

Brenda Wentworth

"I used to get butterflies in my stomach every time I'd drive back to the C-School for years after I graduated. There had never been any place in my life up to that time that I was excited to go to. And still when I walk in the C-School, I feel like I'm going home. It's grounding for me. It's roots."

Roots are important to Brenda Wentworth. She has never known the security of home and family roots, and she continues to struggle with the emotional effects of that void in her life. She started smoking pot and drinking when she was in sixth grade. By the time she was 14, she had left home to escape the extreme abuse of a dysfunctional family.

"I was living with my big sister for about a year at that point and going to school and selling drugs, and I got in a lot of trouble. I was trying to get out of town, and I heard about the C-School."

Brenda became part of a pilot project that led to revamping the 1978 Juvenile Code for Maine. Her counselor contacted the Community School and took her to the initial interview. "I thought, 'What a deal, get my diploma in six months.' I was excited about that. But more than anything else I wanted out of my hometown.

"The goal was to get my diploma almost in a rebellious fashion because my father had said, 'You're no good. You'll never amount to anything. You won't even graduate from high school.' I wanted to prove to him I could, and the C-School seemed like the easiest way to do that. Come to find when I got there, it wasn't so easy. But it was very effective. It changed my life. Definitely changed my life.

"Kids who go to the C-School come in feeling like failures, so the encouragement of the staff is an incredible job. It's a job of trying to get someone to break down barriers that they've built up in order to make changes. You have to break through in order to teach. It's constant vigilance on the part of staff members to get these kids to look inside themselves because they are terrified to do it. I was terrified that if I reached inside there wouldn't be anything there to grab ahold of. And I had to believe them when they told me there was something inside there."

Brenda graduated in the fall of 1978. Ten years later she had earned a Bachelor's Degree in Social Work from the University of Maine and a string of academic awards including Phi Beta Kappa, the President's Achievement Award, and the Ray Dow Memorial Award of the National Association of Social Workers. She is a longtime member of Maine's Juvenile Justice Advisory Group and is employed as a social case worker with adolescents. As part of her job she gives presentations on domestic-violence awareness in the high schools. "I talk to kids about domestic violence and how to confront those issues and empower ourselves so we don't become victims or perpetrators."

Brenda is what every school might well consider a star graduate. But her journey from Community School graduation to her present level of achievement all but broke her emotionally, mentally, and physically. It strained to the limit every fiber of her survival instinct.

"It is real clear to me that I should be dead. I was a junkie, hung out in California, stuck needles in my arms, rode on the back of motorcycles, stared down sawed-off shotguns, and lived an insane life. But I'm not dead; instead I'm a respectable citizen."

How does she characterize herself when she arrived at the Community School? "I was out of control. I was completely and totally out of control. I had no sense of self-discipline. I was self-will run riot. I came in drunk a lot. I was rebellious, had a lot of anger, a lot of confusion. Generally my self-esteem was at the bottom of the ocean.

"But the staff were so committed to helping you succeed. It was the first time in my life anybody had said to me, 'You're a good person. You can make it.' And the C-School was the first place that anybody put limits on my behavior in a loving way and started making me accountable. It was the first time anybody had showed me how my behavior directly affected my consequences, and I started to see the connection between my behavior and the circumstances of my life. The C-School is the very first place I got affirmed as a human being."

Brenda started counseling for her alcohol use during her C-School term but did not go into AA until years later because no one considered her alcoholic at the time. Looking back, she realizes rules were "a little less rigid." She points out that the School itself was still learning how to set up a structure that worked for adolescents. "We helped develop the rules by creating problems that they started to foresee. So they started to develop rules to circumvent those problems before they occurred."

The final month of the term was traumatic for Brenda. She was torn by mixed emotions of excitement at getting out of school and terror at the prospect of succeeding "because it began to look more and more like I was going to succeed at something. I had never done anything from beginning to end."

Brenda was only 15 at the time and didn't know where she was going to go after graduation. She had developed relationships at the School that she "had never known were even possible. I couldn't have articulated that at the time, but I knew I was terrified to leave."

She went back to her family but didn't stay long. "I had changed a lot, and nothing had changed there. That was really hard for me." She returned to the Camden area and started working in the woods with the Young Adult Conservation Corps. She kept in close touch with the Community School and got to know the directors, Dora Lievow and Emanuel Pariser, who had been abroad during her term. Brenda also teamed up with one of the girls in the winter term. After she graduated, they took off for California.

In California Brenda did drugs. "Lots and lots and lots of drugs. That's where I hit bottom. I'd hang out with bikers and became a junkie. The whole time I was out there I got deeper into drugs, started using needles, and got real sick real fast. I was a bummed-out, bottomed-out, drugged-out alcoholic by the time I got back here. Just had traces of memories of people who had been there for me. I was pretty well broken, and I was ready to get sober. I had gone to California at 16 full of life and ready to party and have a good time. I came back 18 years old and broken-spirited. It was pretty scary."

She went to work for the Young Adult Conservation Corps again, started going to AA, and got sober. For the next five years Brenda lived in the Camden area, stayed sober, and stopped smoking pot. In 1982, encouraged by her employers in a community service organization, she enrolled in a developmental program of the University of Maine. It took her a year and a half to reach entry level for the Arts and Science degree. She graduated four years later with a 3.7 grade-point average.

Brenda became a peer counselor in the Onward Program, a work/study arrangement with the university, spent a lot of time studying, and continued to go to AA meetings. She became a member of the Juvenile Justice Advisory Board and is now co-chair of its grants committee. She also worked part-time at the Community School for a couple of terms. Because of these activities, she feels, she was nominated two years running for Phi Beta Kappa which she received in her senior year.

After graduation she went into carpentry and ran a crew building spec houses in Old Town not far from the University. "It was the only way I could survive financially. But after putting on a roof in the middle of December, I wanted to use my degree, so I'm glad to be doing it."

Brenda still deals with the effects of an abusive childhood and has been doing extensive therapy and inpatient rehab work, as she says, "just trying to change some old stuff." She still contacts the Community School when she feels the need of support, but she's not sure she would recommend it to every student dropout.

"I always make an argument for alternative education for almost anybody, but I wouldn't recommend the Community School for everybody. The C-School works for people who work for the C-School. That's its virtue. It makes people reach deep inside themselves.

"And if you reach that deeply inside yourself, you're never going to forget. It's bound to change your life forever. I've not known a student who has gone through C-School whose life hasn't changed immensely from the experience. It challenges people to do that kind of intense internal work. It's not about getting a high-school diploma; it's about changing your life."

Kerrie Highhouse

Kerrie Highhouse is a striking young woman, tall, thin, with green eyes and dark shoulder-length hair. She lives with her husband, John Jones, and their 8-year-old daughter, Jessica, a couple of cats, and "Lady," their springer spaniel, in the house they bought in Big Bear, California. In this warm sun-baked climate where sport is paramount, Kerrie and her husband own and operate a thriving swimming-pool service. The two of them are involved in all kinds of outdoor activity and like to get together with friends to water ski, surf, hike, and play volleyball and softball. For Kerrie life is full of love and work and companionship.

Still, at 28 she is just beginning to emerge from the dark fear of satanic abuse that terrorized the growing years of her life.

Kerrie's parents were divorced when she was in first grade, and she feels that was when "My life started falling apart as a little girl." The third youngest of eight children, she was raised by a sister ten years older. "My Mom—I really didn't see her but probably once a week, and that was for five minutes—she'd run in and drop food on the table and leave again. The men in her life were much more important than we were."

When Kerrie was 15, she dropped out of school. About that time she met a man in California "who kind of took me in. And I ran away to Maine to live with this person. My mother signed me over to this man when I was 15, just gave me away. He became my legal guardian." He had a doctorate in child psychology, was the principal of a public school, and had a wife four years older than Kerrie with whom she rarely spoke. "He did all the communicating between us, all the communicating for me to anyone everywhere."

The nature and degree of the abuse she was forced to undergo from her guardian so devastated Kerrie that only now is she beginning to face the horror she had tried to bury inside. "It was awful. It was a terrible deep dark secret I wasn't ever allowed to tell, and I'd go to my grave before I told."

Her guardian said Kerrie's attitude and actions as a student at the local school were beginning to provoke questions and that she could no longer go to school there. "He was pushing me out, and he knew about the Community School. But little did he know, it was the best thing that ever happened to me."

Kerrie remembers her first interview. "I tried to be on my best behavior. This was my escape. But things weren't right at home. I wasn't right. So I wasn't accepted the first year. But I loved it. I thought, 'This is a safe place,' and I wanted it more than anything. I called every week, I think, to let them know how I wanted to be there so bad and to please consider me for the next term. Once I met the people at the School, I knew that's where I wanted to be. It really taught me who I was, what I could be, that I was a worthwhile human being, and that I was able to accomplish things."

Kerrie filled in the six months until the next term working at a local novelty store where she learned how to run a cash register and handle money. "That was the biggest accomplishment of my life at the time." She continued to live under the control and abuse of her guardian who would not allow her to attend school in the interim.

Once at the Community School, however, Kerrie had a hard time adjusting because of "feeling so different and not being able to tell. We had to go through counseling. He just knew I was going to spill my guts. Every day was fear of my life. I knew that I would die if I spilt what was happening. It was sheer horror. Horror."

But she loved being at the School and did not want to leave for the obligatory weekends home. Compounding her inner torture, the School did not know enough about her home situation to protect her. "They had no idea. This man had such power over me that I couldn't tell. I couldn't tell until I was 25 years old and it was working with my husband. I wouldn't be married if it wasn't for the Community School.

"All the skills that I learned at that school were survival skills for today. Communicating how I feel. Without telling what was going on, I had freedom to say, 'I feel angry.' I never had that freedom before. I learned a lot about myself and my strengths. I saw a whole different picture of the people in the world from the School. Not everybody was like the abuser I had been hooked up with for the past five years. There were people I could trust. There was good in the world no matter what was happening to me. I knew that one day I would be OK."

Kerrie did well in her academics at the School, except for math. And that, she recalls, she passed a few days before graduation. She had a great time on her job working with an all-women weatherization crew for the Human Resources Council.

Three days after her seventeenth birthday she graduated from the Community School and was "terrified" of what she was going to do or where she was going to go next. Rather than return home, she moved in with a boyfriend and his family, but that didn't work out well. Then she lived with a girl who had graduated the previous term.

Finally she did go home. Filled with new-found self-esteem, she faced her abuser when he approached her and for the first time in her life said, "No, you are not going to hurt me anymore." His response was violent. "He commenced to beat the living daylights out of me, threw all my belongings outside, and told me to hit the road. That was a blessing. I picked up my belongings and walked away."

Kerrie went to the School where she met her girlfriend, and the two decided to go to California. They bought tickets on a Greyhound bus and arrived with about $4 between them. For the next year they lived with Kerrie's sister-in-law and worked insulating houses. During this period she met a man whom she married three years later.

"I did have a problem with alcohol and drugs at that time—real heavy. I knew it was ruining my life and I had to stop. I just now have been able to take control. I used it as a crutch for all these years, just to kind of drown myself. When my daughter was born, I knew I couldn't handle drinking. It just tore my life between my husband and I. We just made a pact together that alcohol wasn't it, and we started smoking pot. And that continued for a real long time. Recently we just stopped buying it saying, 'No more; it's a nowhere kind of deal.'"

Kerrie feels that a "whole new world" opened for her after she married. "I escaped from something that I never thought I'd ever get away from. I tried to put everything behind and bury it. And I still couldn't voice what had taken place. In my mind I said it never happened. That was my only way of surviving. But it was something that needed to be dealt with and talked about, and that was real, real hard." Her husband is a source of support and strength in helping Kerrie through this painful process. "It just boggles my mind that we're still married. We communicate extremely well."

Kerrie calls the Community School periodically. She keeps pictures of camping trips and her graduating class—just two boys and herself. "That was the best experience of my life," she says of the School. "My childhood was hell. My life totally was hell except those six months were a whole new wonderful thing.

"I tell my husband I want a vacation and to go there. I want him to meet the people who helped me so much."

3 p.m. to 9 at night at one of the local stores, making
more fun.

utation. I was hanging out with kids that were older than
e way I lived my life. I had money. They were doing the
do—drinking and partying and stuff like that. Kids in
ing that. They were playing basketball and going home
r with Mom and Dad."

learly a kid getting in over her head. There were parent/
ces and one with the school board. In an attempt to keep
e, the school gave her a job in the office. The school's
t Jeanine could do school work if she wanted to, "But I

man year in high school, the state had taken Jeanine from
d she was living with her grandmother who was given
d been in trouble with the law, and toward the end of school
st her temper at a teacher and stormed out of the classroom.
as precipitated when the teacher realized as Jeanine walked
hall that she hadn't been there all term. Before a double
lose to sixty kids, he threatened to have her make up the time
nmer. When he put her behind a room divider in the corner,
nded with strong language, walked out of the room, cleaned
, and left school for the last time. She was barely 15. "I felt
e like a second-class citizen. If they wanted me to live in the
lts, then treat me like one."

ved in the area and knew something about the Community
summer she read the brochure and began to question friends
ne there. "I knew I needed a diploma, I knew I needed an
nd I knew I wouldn't do night school. At night school, you
influences you have during the day."

impressed during her first interview at the Community School
ff members "weren't stuffed shirts. They weren't telling me
I knew that if they weren't going to accept me, I was going to
t term and the next term until they did. My alternative was
t on the streets until I could go because I wasn't going back to
l."

eanine was the youngest student the School had ever accepted.
tudied her academic record and gave her a number of tests before
she could handle the program. Jeanine realized at the start that
e to make some difficult adjustments, but at the same time she felt
re was a curfew, something she had never known. "But like any
you give them restrictions, they feel protected. Obviously there

Scott Skillin

"I'm a dreamer. I like to go off by myself and sit on a rock. I need space time." Scott Skillin's description of himself would appear to be the antithesis of his job in a storm-window warehouse where he works six days a week.

He lives alone in an apartment in Arlington, Massachusetts, occasionally writes poetry, is building a color-slide portfolio, and indulges a lifelong passion for ice hockey. Scott is one of that silent, low-key, and largely unsung brotherhood of Mainers who work off their yaws and yahoos on the ice in competition year-round in communities throughout the state. Scruffy in appearance and with the competence of professionals, these local teams compete solely for the pleasure of the sport.

"I was a big jock all through high school—ice hockey, football, and track. But in my junior and senior year I started raising hell. Got into drugs, mostly to try it, smoking pot and stuff. But I was never much of a drinker."

Even from his preschool years Scott had a short attention span and got bored easily. As he got older, he generally lost interest in school. If a teacher or particular subject bored him, he didn't go to class. He was a couple of credits short at the end of his senior year and left school a month before graduation.

Home life in Scott's case was not a contributing factor. He remembers having a "pretty good family relationship" growing up in Harpswell, Maine, with an older brother and younger sister. His father was a civil engineer and his mother, a nurse and member of the local school board. He had gone camping as a Boy Scout when he was young and later worked at summer jobs on lobster boats and at his parents' restaurant.

"My parents brought us up to show up on time and do our best. There was never any strict pressure from them, like make straight A's. They let us do pretty much what we wanted as long as we kept out of trouble."

It was not until several years later that Scott's attention-span problem was attributed to a minor birth defect diagnosed through a series of medical tests in Boston. He has since pursued courses of study in English and math at Harvard night school, Boston State, and Bunker Hill Community College for several years.

When he lacked the credits to graduate from high school, a friend forwarded a Community School brochure to him. "It sounded like something I wanted to do. I didn't want to go back to high school. It was not for me at that time—a critical juncture for me. I just wanted to move on to new horizons. When I went for the C-School interview, I knew as soon as I walked in it was for me, something I could relate to. I went in with a purpose, to get my diploma, like it was my last chance. It was a good experience for me. It made me more aware of others."

Scott was 19 when he entered the fall term, 1979. "I don't think I had any problems. I can honestly say that. I went in there with a positive attitude. I knew from the start this was the place for me, but I wouldn't recommend it for every dropout."

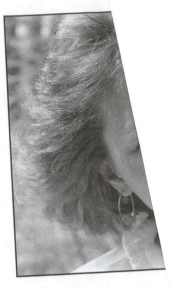

Jea

Jeanine Griffin was wearing a
she stepped up to the microph
Committee. Her long gold hair
at her ears. She appeared poise
members why they should not
from twelve years earlier. Typic

"If it hadn't been for the Con
now." A slight stirring in the audi
comment. Jeanine looks too prop
She is married, has a son and two s
business manager of a workshop f

Jeanine learned early how to ha
support herself. She was just 12 whe
she was in ninth grade, she was wor
her independent spirit. It also kept h
family. And she had never liked scho
getting a lot of guidance at home, and
school—peer pressure, negative, pos
knowing how to deal with that, so I'd

By the time she was in sixth grad
random at best and often proved disrupti

up. Working from
money, was a lot
"I got a bad rep
I was because of t
things I wanted t
school weren't d
and having supp
Jeanine was d
teacher conferer
her out of troub
opinion was tha
didn't want to.'
By her fresh
her parents, an
custody. She ha
that year, she l
The blowup w
into his study
classroom of o
during the su
Jeanine respo
out her locke
they treated n
world of adu
Jeanine li
School. Tha
who had go
education, a
have all the
She was
that the sta
what to do
go the nex
hanging o
high schoo
At 15 J
The staff
deciding
she'd hav
safe. The
child, if

was a piece of me that knew I wasn't old enough to be out alone, yet I was. I was scared probably, and rightly so, I should have been."

She hadn't been at the Community School two weeks when she faced one of the most painful choices she'd have to make. Her boyfriend was moving to Arizona and wanted her to go with him. "I had to make a decision—either go or stay in school. I knew that if I didn't complete the term, I'd feel like a dropout. I'd really feel like a failure. The Community School gave me a chance, a foreseeable chance to accomplish something. And in doing so it gave me a starting point. It allowed me to complete something—start something and finish it. Anybody who drops out of school has a sense that maybe they can't do that. 'Maybe I can't accomplish anything. Maybe I can't finish what I've started.'"

Jeanine finished all right. Even today she says in retrospect the most significant element of her relationship with the staff was that "I trusted them. At that point I needed somebody to trust, and they fit the bill." The Thursday night Group Rap was a keystone of the program as far as she was concerned. It was a time for students to say "what they needed to say. It was a safe place, and we were all together. We voted on things, made our own decisions. We made our own consequences. If we were late for curfew and didn't come up with a consequence, someone else would. So you volunteer to clean the bookshelves or you'd be washing the truck in December."

Jeanine has hiked and climbed in the Maine hills ever since she was introduced to outdoor skills on C-School camping trips. "I appreciate them even more now because I realize they were little mini-vacations I didn't have to pay for."

Perhaps because Jeanine was so young, Dora and Emanuel filled parental roles for her. She still gets in touch with them to talk over a major decision about a change in job or personal problem. "They've shown me that you can be intelligent, but you don't have to be orthodox. Not having to fit into a hole that you don't fit into is freedom of expression. If you did fit, you probably wouldn't wind up at the door of the Community School."

Jeanine is happily married, and her life is full with home, family, and her job. But she's always found time to lend support when the School needs it, even traveling to Augusta to speak at legislative hearings. She organized the School's tenth anniversary celebration, works at the annual fund-raising auction, and has served a term on the Board of Directors. "When I was there, I felt a sense of pride that I was a part of the School, and I still feel that way."

Ed Foster

Ed Foster was the only person at the conference table wearing a suit and tie. The youngest member of the Community School's National Advisory Board, he had garnered within the past two weeks a combination of honors it is unlikely any of his shirt-sleeved elders at the meeting could claim at their college graduations—*summa cum laude*, student commencement speaker, and a full graduate-school scholarship.

After listening to him for a few minutes, it's not hard to picture Ed with a PhD teaching history at some school or university. His presence, choice of words, and easy, chuckling manner of speech project a maturity beyond his age. Board members hung on every word as he sketched a brief history of his personal life.

"School was terrible, and my home life had deteriorated to an intolerable point. I began doing drugs—every conceivable variety. These were turbulent times. When I was 15, I heard about the Community School and hitchhiked up to Camden and banged on the door, and I got in. Finally I just stopped acting self-destructively. I've been in the Army and college and am in graduate school right now. What the Community School gives you is the first step."

Ed's nutshell version of the previous ten or twelve years of his life gives no hint of the emotional struggle and economic sidetracks that marked his tortured path to the graduate-school door. "When I started having problems at school in Bath, my whole future was changed. I knew I wanted to get a high-school diploma and go to college. I knew it deep down inside although I certainly didn't talk about those things. It would have sounded a little strange—here I am proclaiming on the ship going down—so I sort of kept it to myself."

Ed had been an honors student in eighth grade. A year later his grades were "just about straight F's." He was having problems at home and started smoking a lot of pot which he considered a symptom of the problem. "At 14 I was very heavily into electronics and radio. I got an amateur radio license and spent a lot of time learning how to build equipment. When I got to be 15, I guess my main interest was being cool and smoking dope and drinking. I would say I had a substance-abuse problem."

About this time he moved into a place of his own and worked after school and on weekends to pay the rent. His older brother—he had two in school at the same time—had been in trouble, and Ed felt he was following in the wake of his problems with the same teachers.

"I remember one teacher who constantly said that if we didn't work very hard, we'd wind up working for the city of Bath. I was horrified. How many people in class had parents working for the city? And I wondered what he was doing for them. I lost most of my faith in high-school teachers. They didn't understand what I was going through. Of course, I was doing my share of illegal activities, but they more or less thought of me as some sort of criminal."

Problems with the school authorities came to a head when he skipped school for five days to visit a friend in Presque Isle. Disciplinary measures involved Saturday detentions. Ed worked Saturdays, so detentions built up. At a meeting with school authorities, it was decided that he could no longer go to the Bath school. "We were basically finished." It was proposed that he attend a rehabilitation program run by a businessman that Ed had heard "awful things about." In passing, someone mentioned the Community School in Camden.

"I just heard the name—no one told me what it was—so I thought I would check it out. I really did go there completely on my own initiative, 100 percent. I'm not sure how I got to Camden, but I got there, banged on the door, and told them I was Ed Foster and I wanted to go to school there. I talked to someone, and they set up an interview.

"This was 1980. I was accepted, and my brother and I drove up in his Volkswagen. It was about two weeks into the spring term. My room was on the third floor, and they said I'd have to be on time for dinner. I was always on time, but I guess I was exhausted from the drive or something.

Well, right from the beginning I had to explain why I was late. I was definitely the newcomer.

"Academically I think I could have passed all the tests the day I got there. Dealing with authority, I guess, was the problem. I liked the fact that the teachers and staff were very genuine and sincere. I looked at them as sort of halfway between authority figures and peers.

"I got along with the kids fine. I didn't get along with Dora (Lievow, co-director) on a few occasions. I think I had more problems in my personal relationship with women probably because my social awareness was about as bright as a 20-watt bulb. I was pretty sexist. I had problems with my mother, but I certainly never hated women. Problems with women was a recurring theme."

Ed stayed in the Camden area three or four months after graduation, got a job a few miles out of town, and did a bit of tutoring at the School. Although he recalls he was "glad to be done with the School," he was aware at the time it had been a "very important part" of his life and would be for a long time. Unlike many graduates Ed felt no need to call the School for emotional support or simply to touch base. "The whole premise of this Aftercare I didn't feel was something that I really needed to pursue." Co-director Emanuel Pariser called on him to help fund-raise on occasion, and Ed was an articulate and effective spokesman for the School.

"I told them the Community School had given me the tools to do what I did since. I had reached a real roadblock. I was 16 years old; I wasn't fitting into anything. No one really liked me. In the adult world it bordered on hate. So the School gave me a chance to fit in, a chance to succeed at something, a chance to be part of a community. They gave me the basic tools—that piece of paper you need to go to anything. Of all the things that have been positive in my life, I've needed that piece of paper. The Army wouldn't have accepted me. I certainly wouldn't have had the money to go to school; I wouldn't have gotten into school."

Getting the money to go on to college directed most of Ed's moves after graduating from the Community School. He spent a winter washing dishes at the Sugarloaf Mountain ski resort, but there was no snow to speak of, and business was bad. Back in Bath he went to work for a bakery, learned to make quiche, and when that part of the operation expanded to Rochester, New York, he went there for several months until the management changed. Home in Bath again he went to work with a carpenter building his parents' new house. By then he was on good terms with his family, so he moved into a tent on their land and learned something about building houses for a summer.

"All along I was thinking, 'How am I going to get into school?' I was almost a pacifist, but I said, 'I've got to find a service that will give me enough benefits for school.' I went to everyone—the Navy, Army recruiters, Air Force recruiters." The Army had the best deal including a guaranteed tour of duty in Europe. That was important to Ed, partly because some of his ancestors came from Germany and he wanted to see their native country. He signed up and went to Germany where he was assigned as a guard to a nuclear missile site from 1982 to 1984.

About a year after he got out of the Community School, Ed stopped smoking pot and doing other drugs as well. "After I realized this stage was not something I really wanted to be, I just stopped being it. I drank a lot, but I wouldn't say I was an alcoholic. But I was in the infantry in Germany, and that was pretty much our pastime—cruising bars and drinking. I just got tired of it."

With the progression of his life, Ed realizes that his relationship with the Community School has altered considerably. "I'm no longer a high-school dropout. I have four years of college. I've been in the Army. It's a very changed relationship."

Ed is reminded of the German concept of *gemeinschaft* which embraces a sense of community. "It wasn't so important that I always belonged to that (School) community as that I could belong to a community.

"It seems to me in this day and age our communities change rapidly as we move from one part of the country to another. Whereas if I had grown up in some village in eighteenth-century Europe, I would be in that same community from the day I was born to the day I died. There would be that steadiness a lot of people really search for. That's what I needed when I was 16 years old. I needed that steady community, that sense of belonging.

"Of course, I no longer belong to that community because that community doesn't exist. The School has different students, and much of the staff has changed. Intellectually it exists, a steadiness from within. We are born into a family, and the family dies, but we continue on. The fact that we once had that family is just as important. That's part of the life process, isn't it? "

Rhonda Batty

"I got the letter about the book and thought 'Whoa! The book and the Aftercare Program all in one.' I wrote right back."

It had been ten years since Rhonda walked out of the Community School bare weeks before the end of the term with every course unfinished. "Kicked myself out, they said." She has regretted her rash impulse and all that precipitated it many times over the years and felt the despair of squandered opportunity.

But here was the letter asking if she'd like to be involved in the book project and the new Outreach/Aftercare Program. She wrote that she was interested, but she doubted the School would find she had much to offer. After all, she hadn't completed anything at the School and had been out of touch with everyone there for years. She often meant to call or stop by, but intentions slipped away. Now divorced with four children aged 1, 7, 9, and 11, her life seemed worlds away from that once close family at the Community School.

Rhonda is the only former student interviewed whose home setting suggests another time frame. She and her family live in a weathered two-room house beside the road in a rural community. The roof sags around the base of the chimney where a curl of smoke at any time of the year indicates someone is at home. Cujo, the family dog, runs out barking from under the house to announce visitors as they step around several bikes and scooters lying about the bare yard.

Family life is pretty much centered in the kitchen where pots, pans, and the stuff of old country stores hang from the smoke-darkened beams overhead. Rhonda cooks meals on a cranky wood cookstove that supplies the room's meagre heat in winter. Water is drawn from the well with a pitcher pump in the kitchen sink. For the kids' baths, Rhonda heats water on the stove and fills a washtub on the kitchen floor. When she can, she drives to her mother's about 10 miles away to do a load of laundry and take a shower. But more often than not the old-model used car in the yard doesn't run. "The gas tank is rusted out," she explains offhandedly. "I've got another tank; I just haven't got around to putting it on." No challenge ever seems too great. The well runs dry in summer, and the pump pipe freezes in winter. No problem. She thaws what's frozen or hauls water from a spring "just a mile down the road."

But that was not always the case. The Community School presented a challenge Rhonda didn't meet. Not that she couldn't or that she failed, she just didn't want it enough. She was 17 at the time and caught up in a whirl of party-loving friends.

School was never a problem when Rhonda was a youngster. She even liked elementary school. Rhonda grew up in a country area outside Rockland with her twin brother, older brother, and two older sisters. Her father died in an automobile crash when she was about 4 years old, and her mother worked in one of the fish plants. Rhonda took care of people's horses in summer and loved to ride.

But when she got to high school, she started skipping classes, hanging out, and smoking pot with friends. "I'd go to school part of the day just to prove that I was there." She and her twin brother often hung out together, and she dropped out in her junior year shortly after he did.

"I regretted not getting a diploma. I moved out of my mother's about that time—she was mad at me for not finishing school—and moved in with my Aunt Barbara." Rhonda's mother thought it would be good to look into the Community School. Rhonda had not heard of the School before but went to an interview on her own.

"I thought, 'I can do this, no problem.' I started right in at the spring term. I liked it. Some of the rules took getting used to. There was my drinking and stuff. And I was out doing that all over again—drinking and partying. My Rockland friends followed me to the School." During that term the students staged a wild party behind the public high school and created considerable trouble with town authorities for the C-School co-directors.

"I more or less knew that if I didn't smarten up, I could consider my diploma good-bye." Rhonda was doing well at her academics, got along with staff and students, worked at a day-care center, and had fun on the camping trips.

"Why didn't I finish? It was just like high school. I didn't stay away from drinking and partying with friends long enough to finish. I tried to stop drinking a few times. Went to Community Alcoholic Services for a while. But I'd go out with my friends and say, 'I got to get back,' but I'd get drinking and forget about it, about caring, end up being late. Regret it the next day and still do it again. I guess it still never really rung in my head.

"I was told, 'We're not kicking you out; you're kicking yourself out,' which was true when you think about it because Rockland followed me up there. That was my big trouble. If I'd stayed away from people I partied with until I at least finished, I'd have made it. I wasn't living up to my responsibilities.

"I went back to my mother's. Worked down to the fish plant. The Rockland group fizzled out. I just wanted to stay home after that for a little while. Upset? Yeah, after it really sunk in, once I got home and thought about it and all."

In 1981 Rhonda married a merchant seaman she met during the time she was attending the Community School. For the first couple of years they had no place of their own. Then they bought a house in Rockland where they lived four years. Rhonda was 19 when her first child, Tiffany, was born. When her husband was at sea, she worked at various part-time jobs. The boys, Travis and Tyler, were born in Rockland, but when her husband left the merchant marine, they moved to the small house and lot he owned in Hope where Rhonda now lives.

Although the house needed a lot of work, her husband's promises to repair it remained largely that—promises. On weekends they junketed around to country flea markets where he indulged a penchant for antique household relics and tools. It was fun, but $5 salt shakers and $40 circus posters hold little charm for a woman with three kids and no running water.

About the time Rhonda wrote the Community School, the ball and chain around her leg were all but visible. She had no job —"He doesn't believe in it; he's kind of old-fashioned"—no car, no driver's license, and no high-school diploma. "If I looked for a job now and they wanted a diploma or some sort of education or experience in that field, I've got none of that. I'd do anything to get a diploma."

Rhonda became the first student in the Community School's Outreach/Aftercare Program. For a full year she and her tutor cleared a space at the kitchen table and worked together on subjects she had walked out on 10 years before—social studies, economics, history, chemistry, physics, earth science—studying, reviewing, and passing tests. Rhonda revealed a sharp mind, an ability to comprehend and retain what she read. Above all, she developed the power to concentrate despite the distractions of kids in summer and cold that defied the wood stove in winter.

While her divorce was underway, the phone was frequently cut off, and out in the country, often without a car, it was a struggle to get the necessities for day-to-day living. But Rhonda tends to minimize hardship or the burden of the unexpected. Some months after her divorce she took calmly in stride the birth of her third son, Trevor.

Rhonda will soon have her diploma because she prevailed against odds that would have daunted many in far better circumstances. But as Rhonda once said of her experience at the Community School, "You can do it if you try. If you live up to your responsibilities, you're going to make it. But you can't just sit there and wait for it to come along. You have to do it for yourself."

Barbara Nickles

Barbara Nickles is a good-looking woman with a thick mane of blond hair. She appears strong and sturdy, capable of handling herself in tough times. There's been enough opportunity in her twenty-seven years to become quite experienced at dealing with trouble, but Barbara says it's stubbornness that pulled her through. "I don't take no for an answer easily."

Stubbornness with a good measure of determination accounts for several positive moves in her life including her acceptance at the Community School. She was 16 when she first applied. "I was in legal trouble, and someone suggested the School as a way out. Of course, I wasn't accepted for that reason. I got accepted when I was 19 after three or four tries. I just kept reapplying. I couldn't stand the fact that they were turning me down completely, but I always wanted a high-school diploma and planned to get it one way or the other." Little did she realize that she would have to earn it twice.

Barbara's love/hate relationship with academics has marked her entire school life. She disliked elementary school and junior high and despised high school. She was suspended seventeen or eighteen times during her freshman year because she couldn't get along with the teachers.

"I don't think I ever had a passing grade. They just kept pushing me ahead with the justification that I had the potential." The major exception came in the fourth quarter of her sophomore year when she made the honor roll "to show them that I could do it." The rest of the time, she recalls, "I was a disciplinary problem, mainly because I used drugs and drank a lot of alcohol. I lived more for that than I did for going to school; that's for sure."

Barbara worked at a number of jobs after she quit school: fish factories, day-care centers, and state parks with the Youth Conservation Corps at Tanglewood. "It was service oriented. We'd work hard for eight hours a day and drink beer at night in our cabins. Kind of like one big family—at least 150 kids. I went to Rangeley to work, pitched a tent, and did a lot of hiking carrying backpacks and tools. After a week we'd come back and get our paycheck. I loved it."

At the Community School her worst problem was learning to cope without alcohol. Legally old enough to drink during off time, she was confined to the School building for an entire weekend when she came in late one night. "I was pretty ugly. I had a real drinking problem which I didn't know at the time. I just thought I liked to do it, and the biggest thing I missed was drinking with my boyfriend.

"But that was the height of my misery. They really made a lot of exceptions for me to help me make it through the School. At the Group Rap where they lay down all the ground rules for the term at the beginning, I told them I could make it through if I was allowed to have one beer every night. The other students decided I could as I was of age. But it wasn't long before my one 12-ounce beer was one 16-ounce beer and then 1 quart of beer.

"After a while the staff insisted I go to Skyward. I was still in denial about my drinking problem even though they weren't. Had it not been for them recognizing my drinking problem and making me do something about it, I don't think I would have made it through."

Eight years later Barbara was still making it through the School. After the graduation ceremony she confessed to Dora that she had cheated on two final exams. One student had stolen some tests from the office, and a few members of the class copied the answers. The staff was stunned. "I couldn't live with myself. I got a couple of beers in me and had to tell Dora." For the past two years Barbara has studied with a Community School tutor and made up all the work, not just the tests she cheated on but the others as well. "I felt guilty all these years. I knew eventually I would do it. I didn't realize sobering up was the only way I would."

Sobering up was a major struggle. After leaving the School, she married her boyfriend and worked as floor lady in a groundfish factory. She also left Skyward. "I couldn't relate to them. As far as I was concerned, it was fine for them, but for me it was unnecessary." But she was so ill after her third month of pregnancy, she could no longer go to work or drink alcohol. Soon after her son was born, she went back to work and drinking.

"I worked outrageously, sometimes twenty hours a day. I can remember staying for cleanup until 11 or 12 o'clock and then going back for the 4 o'clock morning shift. I liked it." Barbara had a baby-sitter who lived in her building, and except for weekends, she spent very little time with her baby. "I really didn't know what it was like to take care of a baby. Maybe that's why I worked so much. But I knew how to care for it. I knew instantly if it was sick."

When her second son was born a year or so later, Barbara's drug and alcohol abuse had reached a serious stage. She was caught selling drugs, and while she was on probation for trafficking, she was caught drinking precipitated by a suicide attempt shortly after her divorce. "That's why I got caught. They weren't very concerned that I was swimming around in the ocean in the middle of winter but that I had alcohol in my system while I was doing it." There had been other suicide attempts when she was a teenager. "I think the only time I didn't think about suicide was the six months I was at the Community School because I was happy. I really enjoyed the School."

In jail Barbara didn't have a chance to deny her problem. Afterwards she went into rehabilitation for twenty-eight days. For a while she alternately drank and stayed sober. Finally she voluntarily put herself into rehab at Mercy Hospital. "We weren't allowed to watch TV or read any books or magazines unless they were drug- and alcohol-treatment related. We stayed on the fourth floor of Mercy Hospital, and we wrote and studied and found ourselves."

Barbara does volunteer work at her sons' elementary school and is president of the parent/teacher organization. She is chairperson of a group of Community School alumni in her area that does some fund-raising for the School as well as service work for the elderly and handicapped. "Whatever we can do to make a difference in just one person's life is good for the person and for the School."

She goes to individual counseling and AA regularly. For the most part Barbara feels pretty good about herself. Looking ahead, she wants to go to college and law school and then work as a probation and parole officer in a correctional center. "I don't know if I want to work at the one I've been to, but the whole time I was there I wanted to be working there. That was the worst part about being there. I wanted to be on the other side, and I couldn't figure out why I wasn't. But they were aware of it, and they treated me like a human being."

Barbara admits to having ups and downs. "Sometimes I feel like a lousy parent. Certain times in each year—an anniversary, negative or positive—bring me down. So I have to really watch out for my sobriety. Once that passes, I'm OK again. But it's life. I feel hopeful."

Mark Sabatis

Mark Sabatis drives an 18-wheeler all over New England and the mid-west hauling everything from potatoes to Pepto Bismol. Eggs, steel, wood, chickens—his freight is whatever the company ships. He likes being on the road, the changing landscape, seeing country from Miami to Minneapolis. At 27 his body is lean and taut and radiates the strength and energy demanded by long sleepless hours at the wheel. Sometimes he travels thirty-six hours at a stretch, then stops and sleeps for eight or nine before hitting the road again.

"I take catnaps here and there. I have developed time in my body. My body knows when an hour's up. I'll jump up and check the time and take off. That's the easiest way to wake up, or I'd go back to sleep." Mark smiles, his even white teeth setting off his handsome features and black hair.

Mark's father was a truck driver, and Mark went trucking with him for a time before getting his own trucker's certification. He approached his leaders in the Houlton Maliseet band who agreed to finance his ten-week training course at the local vocational technical school. Although the week on the road is often hectic, Mark is usually back in Houlton for weekends with his wife, Brenda, their 7-year-old son, Mark Anthony, and daughter, Ranae, 2.

Mark quit high school for many of the same reasons as a number of students in his community. He remembers the first day of his second year in ninth grade. "I went to my first class, and that was it. The first year I missed seventy-seven days and most of the next year. The only reason I started skipping school was because of parties and other things. That's where it was at."

Alcohol was not as much a problem for Mark as drugs, and he considers himself a heavy user at the time. His first big trouble came with a criminal trespassing charge and subsequent probation, a limitation he was either unaware of or did not understand. At any rate, he dropped out of school in January, ran away from home with some friends, and this time was charged with breaking probation. He found out about the Community School from a pamphlet on his probation officer's desk and commented that it looked like a nice place. "She said, 'Would you go there?' I said, 'Yeah.' She said, 'Hold on,' made a few phone calls, and, bang, I was all set for an interview in February.

"My first impression? I said 'This is all right.' I was expecting an actual schoolhouse, and this was just a regular house. The whole place was pretty cool, the people cool. As for the interview, I was definitely nervous."

While he waited for the outcome, Mark lived at home with his parents, who had taken him to the interview, and his brother and three sisters, all younger. He remembers the moment he heard he was accepted. "I was pretty excited when they called. I was home watching TV that night. I called a few friends and said, 'I'm leaving.'" He entered the School in the spring of 1981.

He liked the School and felt he adjusted to the students and staff pretty well. In fact he enjoyed the whole community. "I made a lot of new friends. I think I knew the whole town in two months." He remembers School trips in detail—hiking Wildcat Trail and camping in New Hampshire and the class trip to New York and seeing Chinatown. "I had a wonderful time on those." There were a few disciplinary problems—coming in late for the most part. "I came close to getting kicked out one time. I was playing a game with one of the teachers and lost. I slammed my hat down and out rolled a joint. I forgot it was there. I got probation for that, got grounded."

Classes went much better for him than they had in public high school. "Your teacher was right there, not a million miles away. I couldn't see the board anyway because I needed glasses, so I tried to figure it out on my own." Mark never complained about it because he preferred to sit in the back of the classroom. With the Community School's one-to-one instruction, he "learned more from them than in a regular high school."

He graduated, but he still asks himself why he did what he did. "I cheated on three tests which I didn't need to. I think about it every year, six or seven times. I told them at the graduation party. I'm a pretty honest person, and I couldn't keep it in. I said, 'I cheated on a test.' I told on other people too and who took the answer sheet. I spilled my guts. That kinda bothers me too. It bothers me to let those other people think I'm a rat because I told on them. I should have let them tell on themselves. I mean to go back and take it over, but it's difficult. I will some day. It's something I've got to live with the rest of my life."

Back in Houlton Mark soon was in serious trouble. He stole two cars right after graduation and was put on probation for four years until he was 21. "I couldn't get hired. Hung out with kids. I was supposed to go in the Marine Corps after graduation, but I kinda blew my future on that."

To lessen his charges in court, he went into rehabilitation in Bangor for alcohol abuse. There he met people his age and "learned things about myself. The first night I got back, there was a dance, and I hadn't done anything for thirty-two days. I was walking up the street, met some friends, and right off quick, 'Hey, I'm back.' The rest was history."

In his subsequent struggle with himself he consciously began to eliminate his associates, but he wasn't quite out of the slough of his despond. At a party a fight ensued, and Mark beat up a man pretty badly. He was charged with two counts of assault. He paid a $45 fine and went to jail for fourteen days. "That was it. After that I said, 'It's time to get my act together.'"

As Brenda served him a late breakfast in the kitchen, Mark appeared to have put some major problems behind him. In sharp contrast, his cousin, red-eyed and reeking, lay stretched on the couch in the living room where the television was blaring at top volume. Mark playfully hoisted his cousin's child to his lap. "His Dad's going nowhere, but I'm going to see to it that this little guy doesn't."

Mark understands all too well the pitfalls that lie ahead for kids in his hometown as well as the challenge he faces to provide for himself and his growing family. Although he is no longer in regular contact with the Community School, he's quick to point out that where the School helps kids the most is "growing up." Then, a tinge wistful, he adds, "It's much easier to be a kid than an adult."

Craig Grant

Maine holds a potent influence over its people—particularly its young, its poor, its deep-rooted natives, and its Native Americans who combine all three. Its power is determined largely by place, an ambivalent force that can shackle or liberate at will.

Northern Maine, where the vastness of potato fields is balanced by the proximity of woods and rivers, provides space and sport to feed a restless spirit as it stifles hope of a livelihood beyond the bondage of mill or potato house.

Houlton, the northernmost major city in the area, is a seedbed of frustration, discontent, and despair for young people in their teens and early twenties. Almost all have worked the potato harvest as children traditionally are let out of school to help. Some have worked in the woods, a high-risk occupation at best. Few have enjoyed either or found any substantial prospects for other available jobs. Low self-esteem is general, and the high-school dropout rate is significant. Drugs and alcohol help many of these young people forget the dark end of their own private tunnel.

Craig Grant dropped out of school in ninth grade. "I was absent a lot. And when I was there, I was absent. School was all right until I got to high school. I didn't like it. Felt cooped up, I guess. Bunch of kids would hang out and do all the things kids were doing. I was 14 when I started getting into stuff."

He had repeated grades earlier and was 16 when he quit school. He feels he had a worse time in school than his two older brothers or younger sister and attributes it to a basic conflict with the teachers. "I didn't like them or their attitude, and they especially didn't like me. And neither one tried on both ends."

If Craig has one obsession in life, it is the out-of-doors. In that respect he is a true Mainer. He loves to hunt, fish, and camp in the woods. And he is thoroughly at home in a canoe in all kinds of water. "I learned to canoe when I was real young. That was a natural thing. I had camps of my own and with friends. We had a camp way up in the woods alongside of a lake 11 or 12 miles out of Houlton. I liked that too much to go back to school."

When he wasn't in the woods, he spent the better part of the year living at home and working in the potato house. After he was put on probation for criminal mischief, his juvenile detention officer told him about the Community School. Craig was not driven to apply out of concern about his drug or alcohol use or any career dream. "I just wanted to make a change as far as getting out of my parents' house. It's hard to make a living up there too." He was accepted and entered the following term. At 17 he had been out of school a year-and a-half, and he found it difficult to keep up academically. "The toughest part was cramming to get good grades. I was in ninth grade when I dropped out, and I had three years to catch up on."

Craig stayed in Camden for two months after graduation to complete his academic work. Fortunately, he kept the janitor's job at the YMCA he had during the term, and the director allowed him to stay in a room there while he remained in town. Craig walked back and forth to the School for classes and finally passed all his tests.

"The School helped me with responsibility like going to work, getting along with people. I got on drinking probation one time, but I didn't break probation. I never went into treatment, but I felt I was getting a handle on things while I was at the School."

Nothing had changed when he returned home to Houlton. The old routine remained unbearably unaltered. Craig went to work at the potato farm and lived at home. Both his parents worked—his mother at a nursing home and his father as manager of a fruit and produce business. Socially, Craig picked up where he had left off and once again got charged with criminal mischief.

"I had to get out of that place. What it was, basically, there was nothing to do—no jobs—and I was depressed over that." After he had been home a while, Craig started going to church again. His mother always attended, and he had gone as a little kid. That's where he met Stacy, who had returned to Houlton after some years out of state. They started dating, and a year later they were married. Life began to move a bit faster after that. Craig got a job with a frozen food company in Houlton with the expectation of being transferred to Bangor.

"I knew I was going to get transferred. That was the basic idea. I wanted out of there." During the interim six months, he worked at three different jobs—in maintenance at a nursing home, as a full-time carpenter, and at a lumber mill. In Bangor he drove door to door selling frozen food, then pizzas, sometimes traveling from Jackman to Camden where he'd stop to visit at the Community School.

A year or two later they moved to Old Town upriver from Bangor, where rents were cheaper. Craig got jobs as a mason's helper by day and a pizza maker at night. He lost no time, however, applying for a job at Old Town Canoe Co. and was hired three months later.

Craig now builds canoes and competes in the annual white-water races on Maine rivers every spring. He and Stacy and their daughters, Celeste, 3, and Alana, 1, live in a trailer in a community not far from Old Town. Craig keeps a canoe on his pickup so he can put in for a paddle in one of the nearby streams on the spur of the moment.

"I'm surprised at the contrast between where I was and here," he says, reflecting on the role the Community School played in bringing him to this place in his life. "I was not feeling good about myself. I wondered if I'd ever make it coming from a place where it was hard to make it on your own, where there was not a lot to look forward to. But they cared enough about you, so you cared about yourself, it seemed. They give you a chance. It depends on what you want." Craig knew.

Jerry Pike

Jerry Pike comes as close to the general conception of a real Mainer as you're likely to find. Independent by nature, a born and bred Mainer is a bit cantankerous in harness, at one with the elements, and confident of his innate ability to do the job. Until he gets his feet firmly planted, that can result in a variety of work experiences at an early age.

Jerry hails from Houlton in Aroostook County, the vast northern area of Maine known simply as "The County." It shares with "The Valley" and "Down East" a distinct identity of people and place. As the French-Canadian heritage is strong in the valley of the St. John River and the sea governs the life of those along its shores, the potato fields and woodlands of The County dictate the fortunes of its sparsely peopled land.

Other than wood or potatoes, the job market for kids graduating from high school in Houlton was meagre to nonexistent. Boredom set in for Jerry, as it did for many others along about seventh grade. He was held back in second grade, and when he had to repeat the seventh, Jerry lost interest. "I think they made a major mistake with me when they did that. My grades weren't that great—on the borderline—but now I was 14 or 15." Despite his grades he had enjoyed school sports and played baseball and basketball. "I did what the other kids did—raised hell too."

Jerry fell into the familiar pattern: skipped school to go fishing or hang out with other kids. Then he started drinking, smoking, and "ended up with the wrong people. I was having some home problems and some school problems, and I hated Houlton. I wanted to venture out." As his parents expected, he dropped out of school in ninth grade when he was 16. "I regret quitting, but I wasn't getting anything out of school, and I felt the age difference with the rest of the class. I was always impatient, and I wanted to work."

Before long he got into trouble and was put on juvenile probation. Jerry's older brother had gone to the Community School, and Jerry had attended his graduation, "but I never thought I would go there." His probation officer and his parents talked to him about it, and he scheduled an interview. "They told me it was going to be hard, but it could be done. I knew I was escaping Houlton, getting a fresh start."

Jerry was 17 when he arrived at the Community School for the fall term, 1981. He found jobs but was too restless to stay with one for more than a couple of months. His restless nature and impatience made it hard for him to live in close quarters with other students. "But I had to live with them because I had to succeed with my mission there. I wanted to get through. That was one of the hardest parts, learning to live with other people. But I loved the camping trips. Everybody got along when we were out."

After graduation Jerry stayed in Camden where he had a job at a restaurant. When he broke his ankle, he returned to Houlton for six months. During that time he was charged with drinking and driving. Once again he realized he had to get away from Houlton and the people he hung out with there. He headed back to Camden and with a friend lived in a tent on a mountain, showered at the YMCA, and ate at his former boss's restaurant in return for little jobs. Jerry worked on a construction crew during the day, then pedaled his 10-speed about 8 miles each night to a job at a beach-front lobster restaurant. He averaged a 60-hour work week that summer. He and his buddy eventually found an apartment in Camden, where he often stopped by the School. He never went back to Houlton.

Now Jerry and his wife Renata have two children and a small house and lot in Rockland. He runs his own business, cuts firewood, and snowplows according to the season. Renata, a vocational-school graduate in culinary arts, has been the chief cook at a local restaurant for several years.

Although he seldom contacts the Community School, he says it "made all the difference in my life. It taught me how to make it on my own, that I had to work, had to learn how to get along with other people, how to be responsible. I felt a lot better about myself. A lot of people were proud of me, of course, all the relatives and Mom and Dad. So that's a boost right there. It's the most positive thing I've ever done."

Judy Fifield

Judy Fifield grew up on a small farm outside Biddeford, Maine, with her parents, a brother, and a sister. She helped get in hay for the animals and wood for the stove that heated the house. But when she was halfway through high school, life became far less wholesome.

At 16 she was an active teenage alcoholic, and in her junior year she dropped out of school. "I was spending a lot of time on drinking, and I was getting into trouble." She worked in factories and at odd jobs, none lasting more than three or four months. Between jobs she hitchhiked, mostly throughout the South—North Carolina, Florida, Tennessee—and back to Maine. She had been out of school for three years when she heard about the Community School.

"I had been hospitalized for suicide attempts. There was a counselor there that I trusted, and she told me about the School. I felt I wanted to change my whole life. I knew I was a good person, but I just couldn't pull it off. I just kept getting further and further down....I felt when I heard about the School, it would be perfect for me.

"I pictured the School out in the woods, and you'd have to chop wood and feed the wood stove, and I knew how to do that. I also knew it would be a chance to start over where nobody knew me, and maybe I could make something of myself...because I had a bad reputation in that small town."

Judy is a shy young woman with tawny blond hair and brown eyes. She speaks softly, her words coming in a rush as she talks about the Community School, and tears well up in her eyes as she recalls the painful and poignant times in her early life.

"When I came to the C-School, I was real scared. When my Mom left— and I hadn't been living with my mother—I cried so hard. Of course I didn't want anybody to see me cry. Tree (staff member Teresa Roth) came up to me and said, 'Are you scared?' And I said, 'no,' and the tears were running down my face. Emanuel was my one-to-one, but Tree was very important to me. She was the role model for me."

The most difficult part of Judy's adjustment to the C-School was getting through each day without alcohol. "That was real painful," she says." I white-knuckled it for the first two weeks. Eventually I did drink and was put on drinking probation." Not long after, she broke probation and was asked to leave the School.

A woman Judy had met on one of the School's community service projects was a recovering alcoholic. She encouraged Judy to enter a twenty-one-day treatment program for alcoholism. "So, under the idea that I had failed in other things, I had nowhere else to go. I was 19, an adult. I went to treatment. I didn't see any other choice.

"My last day at the treatment center, the School asked me to come back, and that was the first time they had taken back a student who admittedly had a drug and alcohol problem. I came back and finished all my tests and graduated. And I never picked up another drink after that. Through all the problems that I was having, nobody had mentioned to me, 'It's your drinking that's causing your problems.' When I went to the School, that was the big issue. It was obvious to them.

"The thing I keep coming back to is this: I never thought anyone would think it was important to concentrate so much on one person and, even though it's hard, to do what's right—like kicking me out. That was really hard. It was hard for Emanuel because he was my one-on-one. It was hard on all the staff. It was hard on the students. They didn't want to ask me to leave just because I broke drinking probation, but they did.

"So the way the School helped me—besides daring to confront me by saying 'That's not acceptable'—they gave me choices, and they accepted me back. The School has never stopped caring about me. That's one of the things I love about the School; there's always somebody there. There was eye contact there. People listened to me. People really cared about me. They set limits for me when I couldn't. That's the way the School has helped me the most."

After graduation Judy didn't want to go back to her hometown and confront the temptation to drink. Instead, she moved two blocks from the School where she shared a house with three other adults. She stayed sober, but her bulimia—an eating disorder characterized by eating and purging—got out of control. It had not been a major problem when she was drinking or in school. "But when the alcohol went away," she says, "the eating disorder became more important to me. I really hit bottom with it."

Finally she went into a treatment center in Florida, the only one she could find that also had the Twelve-Step Program. There she met a woman who ran a halfway house in Tennessee for people with eating disorders, and she asked Judy to come there.

In Tennessee she worked for three years in a long-term residential treatment hospital for adolescents with alcohol and psychiatric problems. For two of those years she worked in an outdoor program called Peninsula Outdoor Village, an accredited hospital and camp.

"We lived out in the woods in a log cabin that we built. I was a group leader and had eight to twelve girls beneath me. We also cleared the land and started building another cabin for a second group, and I eventually ended up working with the second group."

At this stage in her life, Judy can tote up a few solid achievements: She has graduated from the Community School, she's stayed sober and is recovering from bulimia, she feels good about the job she's done with kids at the hospital, and she has learned to handle a kayak on some big southern rivers. Enrolled as an English major at Pellissippi State Technical Community College, she plans to enter the University of Tennessee after two years.

Literature is her passion. "I've always read a lot. Emanuel and Tree have fed me books, 'Read this and read this.' I can't get enough. That's one of the first things we talk about. My latest favorites are Anne Tyler and Alice Walker, and I love May Sarton."

Now married, Judy leads a full, happy life in Tennessee. Most of her friends are recovering from eating disorders, and she feels surrounded by a "strong support community." In the long range she wants to get a master's degree and work at a community college.

"I love school. I thought maybe if I was a teacher I could get to go to school all the time, and I dreamed of teaching at the Community School. I've always been in touch with the Community School. The Community School was my first success, my very first. They never stopped caring for me. They are my chosen family."

Steve Hayden

Aroostook County is the northernmost county of Maine, a vast, sparsely settled land of woods and potato fields, high and rolling as far as the eye can see. Separated by the Saint John River on the north and east from the Canadian provinces of Quebec and New Brunswick, "The County," as it is generally known, could easily contain the state of Connecticut. A boy growing up in a small Aroostook community can look forward to two choices for work after he gets through school—the woods or the potato house. As Steve Hayden sees it, you can die of boredom picking and sorting potatoes, and cutting timber, you stand a good chance of getting killed.

From the time he was in first or second grade, Steve has always felt safe in the woods. He'd skip school two or three times a week and spend whole days in the woods building little hideaways where nobody could find him. Now more than twenty years later, Steve bears the mark of a woods creature: gentle, perceptive, and keenly alert. He's sure he still could find some of those secret places and the "rock museums" he assembled there.

"They couldn't keep me in school. Grammar school, first grade, I hated it. Just couldn't catch on." Steve was the next youngest of fourteen children; number 13 he points out. His ten sisters and three brothers had all done well in school, and he soon felt the burden of living up to them.

Rebellious from the start, he failed first grade, was placed in an experimental class for problem kids before going on to second grade, and was held back again in third grade.

"The teachers were quite lenient, and everybody took full advantage of it. I remember throwing books at teachers and being a wild kid." One first-grade teacher, recognizing he had a reading problem, put a book in his lunch box to take home and keep, saying "This might help." Steve recalls she "made a point to let me know she was helping me steal it, so I liked her. She was on my side. Because of her, I got an A in her class. Later on she was my junior high Social Studies teacher. Academically everything was a statement. If I liked a teacher, I did well. In her class I did well. Some teachers at the Community School figured me out too. Bob (Dickens) was a gifted teacher. He figured me out."

With push from some teachers and resistance on his own part, he somehow made it through to high school. By his freshman year in high school—already two years older than most of his classmates—he had started using drugs. He took up with the son of a local family, and together they experimented with a number of different drugs. Although his parents never discussed it with him, he felt sure they had to know he was heavily into drugs. Even in third grade Steve remembers he and another kid would eat sweet tarts and pretend they were taking pills. When he was 16, he told his father he wanted to quit school, but his father would not allow it. Steve knew he couldn't quit and continue to live at home, so he ran away. But not before he was caught for growing pot, a huge plant he was quite proud of. Since he was a minor, he was assigned to six months' counseling with an intake worker. When he turned 17, the age at which he could legally quit school, he dropped out.

Three years later Steve was living with his parents, working in a potato processing plant, and spending a lot of money on drugs. Late one night in front of the television, he realized that his life was a round of working, watching TV, and getting in a rut. "This ad came on and said, 'Finish high school and earn money at the same time.' I thought, 'Wow, I really want to finish but want to earn money too.' I had thought of going back to school at night, but I was too drugged out to stick with anything like that. A change away from my home setting—I was beginning to think about stuff like that."

The next day he called the Community School in Camden and went down for an interview. "The teachers were long-haired and fit in with my thinking at the time, so I took a liking to it right off quick. I took a test and was real scared I wouldn't pass it, but they took me. They accepted people from 16 to 20. I was 20 years old at the time, a last chance deal. I knew I couldn't sit down in a classroom with thirty students. I certainly was not rich and was not going to pay for a tutor."

Growing up in the woods had taught Steve how to be secretive about his habits, and he had learned from experience how to break rules and not get caught. "But at the Community School, they knew I was getting high. It was pretty obvious. If somebody wants to drink or smoke pot, they can't stop that, but they planted seeds in my head. Like one time they said, 'Do you think you would've done better on that test if you hadn't gotten high Sunday?' And I'd say, 'No, I been doing that since I can remember. No way.' So stuff like that planted seeds in my head, caused me to ask myself some questions."

For the first time in his life, Steve found he could succeed at something. His work experience had been limited almost entirely to working the potato harvest "which doesn't take much brains." But he felt he learned a great deal as a mail clerk at the *National Fisherman*, one of his jobs during the C-School term. Sorting mail, working with figures, and keeping track of money spent were all new skills for Steve.

When he finished the term, Steve stayed around Camden and worked for local painters because he wanted to make a new start, although he kept a close contact with the School. "The School gave me some structure. It was more of a family." His drug use let up a bit because he had to go to work every day. More importantly, he felt he wanted to get rid of it.

Steve had particularly enjoyed one of the School's field trips with Outward Bound. The following year he took a four-week course at Outward Bound's Hurricane Island. "It was real good for me because it helped open me to stuff I thought stunk so bad before—all these college students in the boat. I thought, 'Aw no, I don't want to deal with these people. I think they really stink. They're yuppies. I don't like them.' I get on this boat with them and find out that they learn quickly but that they don't retain real well. I find out that because I have a reading difficulty, it takes a little longer to pick up on something, but once I get it, I've got it. At the end of the course I was reminding them how to tie a bowline. At the beginning they had to show me. I found out a lot about the way people learn and that they are basically all the same."

Steve still couldn't shake his drug problem, and he began to think more about a higher power and how he felt it had worked in his life. He recalled a night years before when he had become really frightened. Even then he had tried to stop smoking and couldn't. He thought it "was worth a try" to appeal to a higher power. "I could hide and pray," he told himself. "No one can see me. It might be embarrassing, but I'll try. I asked for a way I could stop, and the next thing I found myself in the Community School and doing

Outward Bound the following year. But something I understand about myself is that a habit I'd done for thirteen years wasn't going to stop in two or three years. It took four years after that."

After Outward Bound he enrolled in a technical school in Connecticut at his father's suggestion, where he could get hands-on skills without much book work. Unfortunately, the drug scene was so great in the area that Steve became seriously depressed. He wrote the Community School asking for literature on drug use. "What I got from Emanuel was something to keep track of how drugs influenced me from day to day. I soon found out that everything revolved around my drug use. If I'd done a certain drug the night before, it would make me depressed the next morning. If I was happy, I'd do drugs. If I was sad, I'd do drugs. No matter what, that was the center. So it gave me a real good idea that I had a problem. I knew the answer was back at the School."

Steve wrote Emanuel asking if they would take him on as a live-in student who would do the driving and maintenance and work around the School for room and board. The School finally agreed on condition that he go to drug counseling in Rockland. "I had no idea how hard it was to stop smoking pot. The way I feel about the School, they gave me this break. If I was to smoke pot, I'd tell them and leave right then. So I managed to make it that five months." Although he later slipped for a time, he had developed "a taste for what sobriety was like. If you've been using it for a long time, after about three months you feel like Superman because the stuff's finally leaving your system. So I was kinda hooked on the idea of it."

He joined a drug-counseling group that he liked and stayed with them for a year. Not long after, he got into a relationship that taught him a lot about co-dependence. He wrestled with that for a time, then took off on a solo, drug-free road trip across the country. On his return the stress of his co-dependence and ending the relationship led to mental problems. When he became suicidal, he put himself in a halfway house. During this period he began to feel that "a higher power or whatever was a lot closer to me and watched over me more."

For years Steve has dreamed of living in a healthy relationship near Belfast and developing a small business geared more to helping people than making money. He is now realizing that dream. Steve has been drug free for five years. He's settled happily in a relationship and is fixing up a house on 50 acres of land he bought in Belmont.

"Life is a real big challenge to me, and I feel that I'm aware of a lot more than a person who didn't have any problems in the first place. In a way, I feel real lucky."

Betsy Robertson

It was still dark on winter mornings when 13-year-old Betsy Robertson pulled on her barn boots and jacket and went out to feed the hens. There were three floors full of broilers in her father's hen house, each ranker than the next with the odor of chicken flesh and feathers mingled with the night's accumulation of droppings. For the next two hours Betsy lugged buckets of grain and water to the hens, then cleaned the cages on every floor.

She worked the dawning hours of every day, making her way to the barn through sleet, snow, or biting cold—mindful on weekdays to be ready in time to meet the school bus at 7 o'clock for the 40-minute ride to school in Waldoboro. When school was over, she came home on the bus and did the hen-house chores all over again. The next youngest of five children, Betsy was helped out by her sister, Anita, two years older. The youngest member was too little to help, and the two eldest children were living on their own.

Every summer Betsy worked at a camping area her father ran on a small lake somewhat north of their farm. Life was a bit more lively at the campground with the opportunity to swim and use the boats and fish. "From the time I was 14, I practically ran the place for my family." She registered campers, assigned places, and attended to the general running of the area. Her friends often gathered there, particularly on weekends when "It was real easy to get booze; campers would give it to us."

But when summer was over, she went back to the farm and the broiler house. For a young girl just coming into her teens, the prospects for breaking the shackles of premature responsibility appeared bleak. When she was 15 and in the ninth grade, she dropped out of school. But the drudgery of her life stemmed from a deeper source. "I was foolish, and there were family problems too. Both my parents were alcoholics."

Innately shy, Betsy is uncomfortable putting her feelings into words. As a student at the Community School, she dreaded the obligatory student/ staff airing of personal grievances in the Thursday night Group Raps. "I didn't look forward to Thursdays." But now from the perspective of twelve years, she is more confident. Fair-skinned with blond hair, she is a calm, sweet-faced young woman with a motherly manner. Happily married and comfortable in her trailer home, she views the forces that shaped her life in relation to her hopes for her own small children—Ronny, 2, and Samantha, 1.

"I dropped out of school primarily because I wanted my parents to make me go back. I figured it was an attention-getter, but it didn't work. My Dad was concerned, but my Mom was drunk most of the time. My sister quit too. She never went back. Now my little brother has quit. My mother died from alcohol abuse shortly after I got out of the Community School."

As she talks, Betsy keeps a constant eye on her children who are tussling over the plastic toys scattered about the living room floor. Outside the window finches and chickadees flit back and forth at the feeder. After she dropped out of school, Betsy spent two years at home, bored and at loose ends. One night she heard an advertisement on the radio about the Community School and called for an interview the next day. She remembers that she was "frightened" during that visit, but "right from the start" she felt the School was a place she wanted to be.

"I think the biggest thing I was thinking of then was getting out of the house. I didn't want to live at home anymore. That was the biggest thing that got me here." Betsy had been drinking for several years by then and realizes now that had she stayed in the home environment, "It could have become a problem. I don't drink at all now, nothing."

Betsy was 17 when she entered the fall term, 1982. "It helped me on a lot of things—growing up. I knew there was somebody there for me if I needed them." Her one-to-one staff person was Bob Dickens, and she remembers that he was "just wonderful" in the support he gave her, especially when her grandfather died during that period.

She enjoyed the jobs she had during the term: four days a week at a day-care center and one day at the local animal shelter. Strangely for someone who had handled a camping area and taken on a lot of home responsibility,

Betsy had never gone on a camping trip or cooked an entire meal before she came to the School. Home cooking had been confined largely to TV dinners. As far as rules were concerned, she remembers coming in late several times and drinking. "I just didn't get caught." After she left the School, she stopped drinking entirely "for these little buggers," she says, turning her attention to Ronny and Samantha. "I just don't want them growing up like that.

"In many ways I changed a lot when I was at the School. I wasn't a kid trying to get back at my parents anymore. The School seemed like the family I hadn't had. After I graduated, I didn't want to leave the School. I'd fallen in love with everybody. But, I don't know, I almost felt deserted by them when I left—almost. I'm not quite sure. I had no idea what I was going to do."

Betsy did not go back to her family's farm when she got out of school. Instead, she moved in with her boyfriend whom she had met at her father's campground and had been seeing throughout her term at the School. They were married that fall. But she had become so emotionally attached to the School that for a time after she left, she felt somewhat abandoned and harbored feelings of alienation and resentment as a result. The School's current Outreach/Aftercare Program for graduates "would have been wonderful," she says, had it been in place when she graduated.

Betsy's home is located at the edge of the woods in a rural community. Although the family's yellow Labrador has his kennel in the backyard, birds, squirrels, and a number of woods creatures including occasional deer provide a continuing source of interest. For family vacations Betsy and her husband like to pitch their tent beside a Maine lake and fish and canoe for a week or so.

Since she got out of the Community School, Betsy has held several steady jobs and acquired additional skills. She worked at a fish factory for two years, then completed a Certified Nurses' Aide course at the area vocational school. For the following five years she commuted daily to Camden to work with elderly people at the Health Care Center there. Although both her children were born during that time, she took off only five to eight weeks before returning to work.

She left the Center to start her own day-care program and is licensed to take up to six children in her own house. Life for Betsy holds far greater promise than she ever thought possible when she was growing up on the chicken farm. "I can stay home with my kids and still be able to make a little."

John Joseph

Maine has not been kind to its Native-American population. Until recently the Indian Land Claims Settlement, late in coming, excluded some deserving bands. For youngsters growing up on reservations, the struggle to overcome the dearth of opportunity or escape the contagion of drugs and liquor is almost insurmountable. But more insidious, the silent contempt many whites hold toward tribal families affects these children brutally when they enter public high school. It gnaws at their self-esteem and clouds the promise that they can expect equal footing with their white classmates. Many drop out of high school and return to the known but lesser promise of the reservation.

John Joseph is a Petty Officer in the US Coast Guard and is stationed in South Portland. He signed on for a four-year hitch, lives in an oceanfront community a half-hour's drive away, and is married to a girl he knew before he dropped out of high school.

John is a member of a prominent family in one of the smallest Native American bands in the state. The Maliseets are scattered throughout the northeast, but their headquarters are in Houlton, a fair-sized small town where John grew up. He was raised a Catholic with his two brothers and four sisters in a lower-middle-class family. He spent summers from the age of 7 at a Native-American camp near Fort Kent sponsored by the Quebec-Labrador Foundation, the State of Maine, and the state's Indian tribes. At 15 he started working at the camp where he was involved in sports, camping trips, and native arts and crafts programs. In winter he worked on the ice patrol at the community arena. "It was fun. I made a lot of friends—knew a lot of people."

John went through elementary school and junior high with few academic problems. He was elected class president in both eighth and ninth grade and sang in the chorus. But his first love was sports, and in his freshman year he played on varsity teams—junior and varsity soccer, varsity baseball, and junior varsity basketball.

In his sophomore year John's varsity baseball coach cut him from the team without offering a reason. John was upset and puzzled but accepted the decision. One of his staunch supporters—also a coach—was told it was because John couldn't hit, but John's hitting ability had won the championship when he was in junior high. He had suspicions about the motive but said nothing. Later, when the Eastern Maine Championships came up, the baseball coach asked John if he would play. "I didn't want to hold a grudge, so I did. My job was pinch runner because I could run fast; I could steal any base I wanted." In the championship game with the team down 6 to 3, the coach put in another player.

"I believed it was because his family had the right name. It was taboo for a Native American to outshine his white counterpart with the whole community watching. It started bothering me. I lived for sports. So after that I started getting depressed. Then I started experimenting with drugs, smoking marijuana, and from then on things started going downhill."

At the beginning of his junior year, he was told he couldn't play any sports because his grades were down, and they were. John recalls the day his faculty friend and coach had a talk with him and surmised, "You're going to quit, aren't you?" John said he was. His teacher told him then that there were teachers who say, "You're nothing but a typical Indian, whatever that means." John replied that he sensed it all around. That was the day he walked out for good. He felt the hurt keenly because, unlike other Maliseet students, he had been much involved with the school and team sports from the start. And his family took it hard.

"I think the thing that brought a lot of my family down—my brothers and sisters—was the attitude they received from people around town. Certain families always were looked upon as bums. It had an effect on me. I had to get out. My friends were not restricted to Maliseet kids. But ignorance breeds ignorance, and a lot of children had the same attitude."

In less than two months John was in the Community School. He had learned about the School from his cousin Mark Sabatis, a former student, and promptly set up an interview. He was jolted a bit on his first visit: "I expected it would be like a school, and I get there, and it's a house." And some men staffers had sixties-style long hair. He thought there might be something here that he'd enjoy, "and come to find out it was a real good experience."

He cites a number of positive achievements: basic survival skills such as finding a job, taking responsibility, and dealing with other people. John's main problem was learning to control his temper. "It took a long time to get me there, but once I was, I was like an animal. I was a pretty good fighter." Of the eight students who started the term, John was one of three who graduated.

"I liked the School, liked the feeling I got talking with the instructors. They were open. They were honest. There wasn't racism, and that made me feel good. They were willing to talk to me as a person, not as 'Here's an Indian.' That's what I needed. It built up my self-confidence which I hadn't lost completely, but it had suffered. I had a change in attitude when I came out. I felt I had grown immensely as far as my emotions toward other people, and I could express myself in positive ways.

"At that stage in my life I was looking for answers—life and death. I liked to read—history, astrology, metaphysics, anything people now consider supernatural. I was brought up Catholic. I don't agree with everything, but I believe in the teachings of Christ—how to treat other people. The more you learn, the more you grow. I believe the Community School planted seeds in my head."

John returned to Houlton after graduation and worked a year for the tribe as Employment Support Specialist, setting up jobs for tribal members. He taught aerobics and took flying lessons. He would have continued flying, but he had applied and been accepted at the Rhode Island School of Photography. He studied photojournalism and all phases of black-and-white and color photography, won many ribbons, and made the school's Court of Honor in photographic achievement.

When he finished school, he returned to Houlton where there was an opening in photojournalism on the local paper. John applied for the job but was not given an interview. The job went to someone with less training and experience. Once again he went to work for the tribe, this time in the Social Service Department. He also worked in the potato house, on construction jobs, and as a bartender. Finally he got a job through the tribe managing Maliseet Gardens, a large congregate housing unit with independent living units for older people and a small mall in Bangor. "It pays to have relatives in tribal government," John says about getting the job.

But the job was not without a share of tribal politics, and John did not want any part of it. After a year on the job in Bangor, he joined the Coast Guard. With a couple of years in the service behind him, John has freed himself from the racist wounds that marred his youth, and he feels good about the course he has set.

Dwayne Socabasin

There's a chill, raw edge to the air blowing in from Passamaquoddy Bay, but it does not permeate Dwayne Socabasin's trailer. He's wearing shorts and a T-shirt as he sits in front of his color TV keeping track of several pro-football games simultaneously. Dwayne, Jr., 2, and Sheena, 5, climb over him in the big chair and slyly eye the stranger who has come for the night.

The room reflects the special significance his Passamaquoddy heritage holds for Dwayne. Photographs of family members in ceremonial regalia are propped on book shelves along with Native American beadwork and basketry. On the wall behind his chair a framed velvet painting of an American Indian chief in headdress is flanked by a rainbow-colored blanket and two Native American good-luck shields. The wooden figure of a woman, her outstretched arms carved like eagle wings, forms the base of the table lamp.

For the past couple of years, Dwayne has been assisting a tribal language instructor in the reservation's elementary school. Although many members of the tribe speak the native language, Dwayne is one of few who also read and write it. "I'm not saying how good that is," he says, "but that it's sad that no one else does." He learned the language as a child from his parents and elder relatives, particularly his grandmother. "I keyed in on it because I was more interested than other kids." Now he teaches his own children, often pausing when he's talking with them to pronounce the word in Passamaquoddy and ask them to repeat it.

Dwayne's life looked far from promising just a few years earlier. When he was a seventh grade student in the school where he teaches, he started dealing in drugs. "I didn't enjoy school at all. I had a lot of friends and that too was a problem. I wouldn't say I was a class clown, but I was always trying, you know, to get the kids going."

Dwayne started high school in Eastport, a coastal community separated by causeway from the reservation. But the change of school and environment did nothing to motivate his attendance or diminish the drug habit he had begun in elementary school. He dropped out before the end of his freshman year. For the next several years he didn't work; he sold drugs.

"The thing is with drugs, I thought at the time, when you sell drugs you do have a certain amount of power. You got friends, you got money, you've got everything that you think is great...until you get to the point in life where it's not worth it."

Dwayne was one of ten children in what he terms a dysfunctional family. His involvement with drugs was not without precedent. "It's a family disease—drugs, marijuana, alcohol. It had been in my family for a long time." Dwayne, however, never used alcohol. "I don't even know what alcohol tastes like. I'm glad because I'd probably be a lot worse off."

He heard about the Community School from a high-school counselor who had been trying to locate an alternative school for him. Dwayne liked the sound of the School from the brochure the counselor gave him. But when he arrived for his first interview, he thought, "What the hell am I doing here? It doesn't look like a school at all."

Even so, he sensed there was something right about it for him. "I realized they would teach you about responsibility: basic life skills that you don't learn in high school like getting up in the morning, cooking, going to work—daily living skills that you have to acquire eventually."

Dwayne had been living with a sister and for some years had been answerable to no one but himself. At the Community School he soon faced problems with authority—"people telling me what to do." He also had some difficulty relating to the other students. In a residential school where staff and students live in close quarters, it soon becomes imperative to respect another person's privacy and personal space. It also had been some years since Dwayne had been in school, and the academic part of the C-School program presented a real challenge.

But there was a bright side too. Dwayne is quite verbal and didn't mind the weekly Group Rap sessions. Camping trips, recalled with mock groans by some graduates, put Dwayne in his element. He loves sports and plays on the reservation's ball teams. The camping, canoe, and climbing expeditions were among his most enjoyable experiences at the C-School.

"But the turning point for me that really opened my eyes was about responsibility. That really sunk in. Being responsible for yourself, paying the rent, going to work. You got to grow up and smell the coffee."

During the term Dwayne worked for a woodlot operator, learned some skills from a custom woodworker, and apprenticed to an oil-burner service company. By the time he graduated, he had paid all his bills and had money left over. He had some tests to finish but completed them after several years. The only other graduate that term was Debbie Pearse, indicating an unusually high attrition rate for any C-School term.

Despite his diligence as a worker and enthusiasm for outdoor activities, Dwayne continued to use marijuana during free time at school. When he returned to the reservation, his drug use increased.

"I got back in the same scene again, the same old thing. I guess I was running downhill again. I started losing jobs, started having that same attitude of not caring. It withdrew me from my family, withdrew me from a lot of things. I went to jail a couple of times for drug trafficking, not long, but that really didn't turn me around.

"I knew that it wasn't the type of life I wanted to live, but this was all I ever knew growing up as a child. I never knew anything else. All I knew was how to smoke dope and how to sell dope, and I was successful at it until I got busted, you know. But this was more or less the type of life I was exposed to. I never thought there was anything else beyond that.

"One day I finally decided I needed help. So I went to get treatment, went to rehabilitation." Dwayne spent over a month at a rehabilitation center in Bangor. It was a trying period, but he stayed with the program because he knew it was something he wanted to do and had to do.

"After I got out of rehab, it was difficult at first, but I had made up my mind that I could find something better, that I could be a positive asset or positive role type doing something that I loved to do—the language."

He approached the Tribal Council and presented a proposal to teach the Passamaquoddy language to all classes in the elementary school. "They knew I was qualified to do it, so I got the job." Dwayne works as an assistant with a Passamaquoddy teacher who speaks the language but does not read or write it.

Passamaquoddy language and culture is now the motivating force in his life. Dwayne has organized a student dance group and stages plays he translates from English texts for his students to present for community audiences.

Dwayne knows all the tribal dances and teaches them to his children. He is a striking figure in his ceremonial regalia and a prominent participant in events during the tribe's annual Indian Days celebration. Dwayne, Jr., enchanted spectators with his performance of the traditional Hunter's Dance when he was only 2 years old.

In a further effort to preserve the native culture, Dwayne is videotaping senior members of his own family as well as elders of the tribe. "I try to get as much history of the Passamaquoddies on videotape as I can, just to document everything. I figure ten or fifteen years down the road nobody will know anything about the different legends of the Passamaquoddy, so I try to get as many elders as possible on videotape because they are slowly dying."

Dwayne has been clean since he left rehab. He is an active and contributing member of his tribe and enjoys a degree of leadership among his peers on the reservation. He indicates that the sense of responsibility he learned at the Community School is ingrained in his daily life. "Right now I can say that things are going a lot better than they ever have as far as my job and things at home."

At 25 Dwayne gives every indication that he will be prepared to fill any role in tribal affairs that may unfold for him.

Debbie and Dennis Pearse

Debbie and Dennis Pearse live in a trailer with their two children on Youngtown Road in Lincolnville, a country community about 7 miles from Camden, Maine. Although they own a trailer on family property nearby, Debbie says, "It's 8 feet wide and 51 feet long—kinda too small with two kids, a dog, two cats, and a hamster," particularly in the long, confining Maine winter.

Their present trailer is roomier but costs $350 a month to rent. It's less than a quarter mile down the road from the house Dennis grew up in with four brothers and a sister and where his parents still live. Both he and Debbie are graduates of the Community School—Dennis in 1981 and Debbie three years later.

Dennis has worked in the woods with chain saw and skidder from his early teens. He knows the trees and the properties of wood and would rather work in the woods than anywhere else. "I quit high school in my sophomore year because I wanted to cut wood. That was the whole reason.

I couldn't sit in a classroom and enjoy myself. I hated to sit; I wanted to move, work, cut wood."

Dennis knew all the students at the Community School because he liked to hang out in Camden. One day he was sitting in the park with a friend who said she was going to put in an application at the C-School. He went along and applied too. "I got accepted, and she didn't. I got my diploma March 20, 1981. I loved it. I'd do it again." After graduation he stopped by the School often and got to know the students in every term.

Rugged and rumpled in appearance, he is never without the felt hat he wears indoors and out. "I met Debbie because of my hat. I'd left it at the School, and when I went to get it, she was there."

Debbie remembers the very moment. "I was out playing basketball when he came in the dooryard, and I heard Dennis asking who this new girl was anyway. They said, 'Debbie Abbott.' We just stood there, you know, and I said, 'Well, wouldn't you like to come into the School with us?' And he said, 'Sure.' And we just started being friends. After that we'd go out, have a good time. Of course everybody knew Dennis. He asked me to marry him when I was in there. Eventually we got married in August, you know, 1985. Been married almost six years now. Two kids."

Debbie is a strong young woman, open and direct without a shred of pretense. But one senses an inner restlessness that she struggles at times to keep under control. She and Dennis are good parents and appear to be understanding of each other and mature in their relationship.

In summer Debbie works part-time cleaning at a tourist motel and is a diligent and dependable worker. But the pay is poor, and the hours are unreliable. She would like to take nurse's training someday so she can work with elderly people.

Debbie was born in Belfast, a coastal town about 20 minutes' drive from Camden. By the time she was in first grade, the state took her away from her mother and placed her with a foster family in Bangor about 40 miles away. It was a well-to-do family with thirteen children and a live-in housekeeper, and Debbie lived with them for eleven years. "It was great. You could share each other's clothes, share your secrets. It was really good."

When Debbie left the family, she decided to try living with her natural mother again. But she found "We just kinda bickered all the time. My father was never around, you know. They were divorced, and she was trying to raise six of us. I never held it against her. I had grown up in a different life, and it was kinda hard to get back into her life."

After an unsatisfactory time in another foster home, Debbie wound up living with an aunt who sent her to a Christian school. "I didn't mind, but it just wasn't me. I was 17. There was a lot of things I had to learn 'cause I was such a rowdy teenager, you know. I knew exactly what I wanted to do, and nobody could tell me any different."

Debbie's social worker told her about the Community School and took her down for a trial night. "When I got there, I saw Emanuel, and he sorta looked like a hippie to me. And I thought, 'Jeez, hippies.' You know, long beards, long hair. 'I don't know if I'm going to like it.'"

Next morning she had her bag packed, but the staff said her social worker couldn't come that day. Debbie, downhearted, realized the choice had been made for her. Fortunately, Bob Dickens, her one-to-one staff member, was on duty the following weekend.

"He's a great guy. I really like Bob a lot. He took me sight-seeing down to Rockland—walked out to the lighthouse, you know. And he took me out to dinner and different sight-seeing places—mountains, you know. He was my counselor, and it gave us more or less time to get to know each other, become friends, which we did. We had a good time that weekend. I really enjoyed it (the School) a lot. I was there two weeks when I met Dennis." And Dennis adds, "We been together ever since."

"Dennis thought I was an alcoholic 'cause I liked to drink. It was in my family. But I had this habit that I had to be drunk. I couldn't feel good just having one drink. I was 18, and I was really confused, you know.

"So Bob and I would sit around, and we'd talk a lot about it. I got on drink probation. That helped me. I finally sat down and figured it out. I don't need to be drunk to feel good or to know what I want. And, of course, I was working with the elderly people up to the Camden Health Care Center, and that made me feel good—doing something for somebody else. Always enjoyed the older people, anyway.

"So I really enjoyed it there. They really helped me think. I feel so strong today, you know, like my feet are on the ground and I know exactly what I want, you know. Just that I really have to get out there and get it. I learned so much going through there. Before I went in, I never had to cook, and that was something new—cooking for all the kids. They taught me my responsibilities. You work, keep up with chores, learn to budget your money. I felt more grown-up than the normal teenager."

"You have to," says Dennis. "What makes the C-School easier to handle is they're just like a family." He worked in the woods for a couple of years after he graduated, but a series of job-related accidents resulted in months of unemployment and family hardship. He flipped a toggling board while he was stretching hides at a local tannery and broke his wrist in three places. The accident precipitated a streak of further injuries, operations, sick leaves, and layoffs. It required two subsequent operations—without medical benefits—to remove the pin, replace it with a screw, and fuse pieces of bone from his hip. It also entailed long drives and longer waits for hospital and doctor's appointments.

"It got to be too much," Debbie recalls, "two kids and staying home all the time. I got my sister over and said, 'Keep them outdoors. I don't care what I do, but I'm going to have a job at the end of the day.' I got the help-wanted ads and the yellow pages, and I did. I got a job cleaning around a hotel. I wasn't making a whole lot, but it was money.

"After that I started climbing up, making good money, you know. And this was all when he was laid up. And we bought our trailer with his income tax return that year. So with my little money, we managed to get by. Of course we had to go down and get food stamps—a little bit of help like that."

"It was a predicament that I never intend on being in again," Dennis says. He later found less physically taxing work at a machine shop as a pipe tapper and became quite skilled at the job. The shop manufactured parts for military machines including the Stealth bomber, but with proposed cutbacks in the defense budget, Dennis was laid off. He now intersperses periods of unemployment with seasonal jobs in the woods in winter and landscaping in spring and summer.

Whatever his occupation Dennis is endowed with an enormous capacity for enjoying life. Like many rural men in Maine, he's a tinkerer. Some part of every day he's under the hood of his aging Suburu coaxing life into the engine. He typifies characteristics associated with the native Maine man: independent, resourceful, at home in the natural world, the hills, and woods. He fishes but unlike many Mainers does not hunt. "I can't shoot a deer." Both he and Debbie love seeing the wild creatures that frequent their area: moose, coyote, an occasional eagle, even, both are convinced, a mountain lion.

Debbie left several courses incomplete when she graduated from the Community School program. She always meant to go back and finish, but with the birth of Nicole and then Shannon and coping with Dennis's injuries and unemployment, time slipped by into years. Ever since she cared for her own grandmother, Debbie has wanted to get Nurses' Aide training to work with elderly people. A high-school diploma was an essential first step. When her daughters started preschool and kindergarten, Debbie signed up with the Community School's new Outreach/Aftercare Program to complete her unfinished work. She had been out of school six years when she started home sessions with a School tutor in early spring of 1990.

At times during a year of twice weekly sessions, the hurdles seemed insurmountable. When the kids were sick and the fuel tank leaked and the gas ran out, Debbie cooked on a one-burner hot plate until they got enough money to pay the bill. If anything, adversity seemed to strengthen her determination. US history, politics, and economics fell behind her with the passing months. In spring, 1991, a special graduation ceremony was held at the Community School for Debbie with her whole family in attendance. With perseverance and optimism she had opened the way for herself.

Jennifer Thomas

"I have been sober since January 8 of this year, and this is the longest stretch I've ever gone without getting high since I was 12 or 13." It was the third week in February, and Jennifer Thomas, 22, sat at ease and self-assured while her 3-year-old son Richard pushed his toy cars around the living-room floor. The lack of clutter and the sparse but attractive furnishings suggest a domestic serenity in stark contrast to the past eleven years of her life.

Small, slender, with expressive dark eyes, Jennifer talks without hesitation, her vivid choice of words painting scene upon scene of a child desperately trying to find her footing in an irresponsible adult world. Born in New Mexico where she spent her early years, she fondly remembers her family's six-week Winnebago trip across country to the farm her parents had bought in Maine. When Jennifer was 10, a few years after they settled on the farm, her parents got divorced, and her father remarried. After he left, home life lost the stability it once held for her, and she began to stay away from home as much as possible. "That included hanging out with people a lot older than I and drinking and doing drugs and whatnot."

Jennifer and her brother were living with their father and stepmother when he died three days before Christmas the following year. Her brother went back to their mother, but Jennifer stayed with her stepmother who had a new baby. "I just wanted to be there. It's where I had been with my father, so I wanted to be exactly where he was at. It was hard. It's taken me a long time to deal with Christmas trees."

After her father died, her stepmother suffered a prolonged emotional breakdown, and for the next couple of years, Jennifer bounced around from her stepmother's to her mother's to foster homes. "My mother had taken up with another man who didn't like me at all, so that's where the foster homes came in." During the years she was 11 to 15 there were few, if any, constructive influences in her life. Parental guidance from mother or stepmother was permissive at best.

"By the time I was 13, I was allowed to smoke pot in front of my mother. She bought me a fifth of brandy at Christmas and let me have cigarettes at 12. My stepmother got me into smoking pot. She got the Winnebago, and we had gone to Florida together, then came back and went to Colorado. I thought it was wonderful. She let me drive, and I was just 12. She had this pot plant that had been in with the tomatoes back of the house in Belmont, and when she was driving I would roll, and when I was driving she would roll. I got into the real escapism of marijuana at a young age."

The euphoria of the road soon dissipated before the harsh reality of undisciplined adult company in Colorado. Jennifer went to school there, but whatever influence it may have offered was overwhelmed by the social behavior of the adults around her. "I remember the first time I brought a friend home from school and walked in the door and my stepuncle and my stepmom were smoking dope. And I thought, 'Gee, I got to get rid of these kids I'm collecting.' I was hanging out with my stepmother and her brothers, and there were no kids in my life. I was hanging out with a bunch of adults and doing adult things."

The situation deteriorated for Jennifer when the uncles began to show her attention in an "unhealthy sort of way." A rift with her stepmother developed, and Jennifer returned to live with her mother and brother. She failed eighth grade but persuaded her mother to put her in ninth grade in another community. There she lived with a teacher—"a structured place. Got breakfast. It was wonderful." She felt the teachers cared, and she passed everything.

"But my priorities were all screwed up. I was swinging into my teen years, and everything I had been taught about love and relationships was backwards. I'd become quite dependent on men for my self-worth, always going out with somebody who was a lot older than I. I was living with one guy when I was 15 who was 27. That's kind of the way everything went."

Jennifer had heard about the Community School from kids who had known kids who went there. She called and went for an interview but was too young. "The minute I got old enough, I called them. My mother didn't want me to do it, but I got accepted in the spring term, 1984, and I got the only single room. I was real happy about that."

She recalls that she arrived with her defenses up. She kept her one-to-one staffer at arm's length and continued drinking and smoking pot. Drugs did not create as much trouble for her as her involvement with a local fellow. "The staff saw how self-destructive I could be when I was in a relationship. My dependence on men made me feel better about myself. When somebody was showing me quote unquote love, that was the most important thing at the time. That just wiped out everything else."

Jennifer was late to everything. She finally was put on late probation which meant dismissal from the School for being late one more time. "I was exactly one minute late coming in from downtown one night, and it was up to beloved Bob (Dickens) to call it, and he booted me. I was devastated. I had one more month, and I screwed myself right out of it. If I'd just run that last stretch, I'd have made it. But my priorities weren't there. I was meant to learn something by this." She returned to the School the next summer and finished the month's work. The following winter she returned to fulfill a required camping trip, but she still owed on her room and board. She paid that and got her diploma in 1989.

Jennifer never had trouble getting a job; keeping one was the problem. This was directly related to her drug use. She "came to terms with the fact that I was a drug addict" while she was at the Community School. But it wasn't until a relationship blew up and she lost control that she called a former counselor for help. He placed her with a sober woman who introduced her to the Twelve-Step Program. After some months she returned to Camden and started partying again, but the seed was planted. "Once you've been in the Twelve-Step Program, you never have guilt-free partying again."

About this time Jennifer got pregnant and returned to the woman she had lived with earlier. "I said, 'If I'm going to make a decision about a life— a decision of this magnitude—I want to do it sober.' So I went into rehab in March '86." When she got out, she elected not to go to her mother's and moved in with a 34-year-old fisherman where she stayed during the rest of her pregnancy. Two weeks after Richard was born, the man said he wanted to live alone. Jennifer moved a couple of times after that—once to a house where all the tenants were sober—and took care of Richard with help from the government's AFDC program. "My son is and always will be number one, and no one ever will come between us."

Periodically she got in touch with the Community School because she was interested in "bringing back the kind of acceptance" she found there. But after rehab her problems seemed to grow worse. She went to Florida, married a man there, and for the next year lived a chaotic round of drink and drugs. "I got introduced to crack and found out how unmanageable life could be." It was the first year of Richard's life. She had a nice apartment and a new car her mother bought and "blew it all out the window. I came back with nothing, owing dealers hundreds of dollars, not even my self-esteem intact."

Then Jennifer blacked out driving one night and lost her license. "It was a blessing in disguise. I haven't had a drink since that night." Now divorced, she lives with her son in South Portland, is still in the Twelve-Step Program, and hopes to get an Associate Degree in Social Service to work with emotionally disturbed children.

"The Community School and the Twelve-Step Program had a major impact on my life. The School taught me a couple of things that the irresponsible side of me wishes it hadn't. It brought me face to face with my addictions. I couldn't deny them anymore. It showed me that I had choices. I had to take responsibility for my actions. They taught me life skills. I knew how to get money and how to live on the street, but I didn't know how to accept responsibility for myself. I didn't know how to take control of the things that I could, and I didn't know how not to control the things that I couldn't. I feel better about myself now than I ever have."

Reaching Out
1985 - 1989

In 1985 I was asked to join Maine's effort to implement the Education Reform Act. This was the School's first involvement in public policy-making, a role which would grow considerably in the next decade. The following year a task force on Truancy, Dropout, and Alternative Education was formed, and I joined it. My role as the School's interface with the larger community was beginning to take shape.

Dora continued part-time, primarily as an administrator, and began doing consulting work for a battered women's program. Four full-time staff took on a wide range of responsibilities from direct student work to administrative duties. With the help of our first foundation grant the School developed a four-year plan that involved more extensive fund-raising and the development of a pre- and aftercare program.

Academically the School was stretching its guidelines: We accepted students with under-sixth-grade reading levels and major math blocks. Under the able direction of Bob Dickens we explored and created ways to determine individual learning styles and paid more attention to enhancing the learning process for each student.

The program developed a more differentiated approach to all levels of learners. When students easily passed our competency tests, we used contracts and special-interest curricula. For students who were far behind in basic skills, we spent a great deal of energy on de-traumatizing them from the effects of previous school failure and finding materials that would play to their learning strengths.

In the interests of bringing form to the process of change at the School, we held "visioning days," day-long think sessions in which the entire staff would attack problems of greatest concern at the time. An agenda from one visioning day in 1985 illustrates the breadth of the topics covered: "Exploring our (staff) roles in the organization. Has Group Rap become too staff oriented? How do we handle/react to sexual feelings on the part of students and staff? What kind of standards should we have for interpersonal behavior at the School?"

In the fall of 1987 the program sustained one of its most devastating blows: Dora and I, the cofounders and co-directors, separated, and the program lost a key staff member. Although Dora and I agreed to continue, working in shifts which did not overlap, our role as joint "parents" of the program was irrevocably changed. Tom Dilibero, our first student, called in anxiously to see if the School would continue. Everyone wondered how such an unexpected and radical departure from the past could work.

To reduce the possibilities for friction and conflict between us, we took on separate responsibilities. Our role changes didn't seem to matter much to new students as they had no past to compare it with. Former students held their breath and awaited the results. For the two of us it was an excruciating time, a time to learn a very different way of working together than we had ever envisioned.

The first year following the separation was rocky. Two volatile terms added to, or perhaps reflected, the emotional state of affairs which had become the substrate of life at the School. Two of our consultants, Bill Halpin and Paul Lipman, helped guide us all through these uncharted waters. As always, staff meetings provided a forum for us to reflect on and grapple with the changes.

Paradoxically, this year also encompassed our first organized effort to effect some programs for the parents of students at the School. Parental involvement had previously been difficult to encourage because many families lived more than a hundred miles away. Family Days were formalized with the advent of the Outreach/Aftercare Program which was funded in 1988. Parents began to have direct access to the School as a support for themselves. For some parents, Family Day was their first experience with an institution which did not blame them for their children's problems.

In 1986 a second wave of the education reform movement swept the country. States began to pay attention to dropouts, truants, and unconnected schoolers who were to a large degree ignored by the first wave. The task force that I had been appointed to pushed through legislation in Maine that established the Office of Dropout, Truant, and Alternative Education, and a permanent advisory board of which I was a member. The School's license was fully restored, and schools all over Maine started investigating alternatives for their disenfranchised students.

In 1989 the School created a Development Committee to work on funding issues that continued to make the operation a year-to-year financial question mark. We assembled a National Advisory Board to help bring the School's experience and model to a larger audience. I took a sabbatical from direct student work to pursue these efforts, and Dora returned full-time.

With interest in alternative education increasing, the time seemed right to begin working on a book about the School. We had lived through sixteen years of alternative schooling with students who had demonstrated an extraordinary capacity to begin taking charge of their own lives and who had many stories to tell. We were convinced that people needed to hear them, to understand the students and their journeys better, and to see how, in the words of one student, they had worked to "not just have their dreams be dreams, but to make them a reality."

Terry Dolloff

Readfield is a small rural town less than an hour's drive from the Maine state capital at Augusta. Route 17 slices through it on its way across the midsection of the state, and the northern end of Lake Maranacook stretches beside it on the east. Terry Dolloff grew up in the Readfield area with his sister and two brothers. He was barely three years old when his parents divorced. "I really don't remember living under the same roof with my father when I was growing up."

Terry went to elementary school in Readfield and then to Maranacook Junior High. With the lake nearby he became a competent swimmer and water skier. But by the time he was 13, he had gotten into problems at school "because of grades and skipping and raising hell." It was decided that it would be better for him to live with his father in Portland and go to school there. He finished the last two months of eighth grade in the city and then went to Deering High School.

In Portland he started drinking and doing drugs—"the whole scene pretty much"—and dropped out of school at 16 in his junior year. He lived off and on with his father, didn't work, and for the most part "bummed around with a bunch of kids." Subsequently he got into some legal problems.

Terry's uncle, the principal of a high school not far from Camden, told him about the Community School. His father encouraged him to look into it, and Terry made the initial contact and was interviewed by a staff member. "It was kind of a scary thing, all new, but I must have been fairly impressed because I pursued it. But I didn't think I would have to wait at least a year." Periodically he called the School to ask when they were going to accept him.

With time on his hands Terry began to drink more heavily. "I knew I had a problem, and it wasn't going anywhere fast, so I moved back to this area and stayed with my mother." He felt he was making progress and was doing well for awhile. Then he slipped back into the old pattern of drinking and hanging out. Finally, the C-School called to say he was accepted. "I was pretty excited. I didn't want to go, and yet I did. I had to do something." He entered the spring term, 1985.

"It was a difficult place. There was a lot of pressure there living with seven other people, going to school with them, doing things at the same time. I always did well in school when I wanted to. It was not a matter of not being able to do but what I wanted to do."

His drinking caused problems, however, and he was almost put on drinking probation. "That was my toughest time. One little time they smell it on your breath—just get caught once—and you're out, but I managed to get through by the skin of my teeth." Terry got his diploma and stayed the following year in Camden working for the landscaper he had worked for throughout the term. During the year he visited the School on a regular basis. "We had drawn quite close at the end of the term. That's where my life was for the past six months. It was difficult to move away."

Terry feels the School's greatest impact was to get him started on resolving a problem. He now lives in North Monmouth where he works for a construction company. He is involved in a serious relationship and is looking forward to the birth of their first child.

Lori Davis

In some respects, the very name of the place where Lori Davis grew up conveys the nature of her childhood—Back Cove. Out of the mainstream, isolated, unnoticed. Throughout her school years the physical character of the place she called home affected her social and emotional well-being.

Back Cove is located 6-1/2 miles from Waldoboro, the area's town center. But youngsters from Back Cove were bussed to elementary school in Friendship at the opposite end of the peninsula. Distanced from the place where she felt she belonged and shunned as an outsider where she spent every school day, Lori felt friendless, unwanted, and desperately alone.

Since she was 1 year old, Lori lived with her parents and two older brothers in the farmhouse on Back Cove. Her mother worked in canning factories wherever she could find a job; her father was bedridden with heart disease. "All I can remember is him being sick in bed. I don't remember him as a healthy person. It was always a strain. He had Social Security, but money was kind of tight. My mother didn't drive, so I was kind of isolated. It was either school or home, and that was about it."

If anything, life changed for the worse when she went to high school in Waldoboro. When she was about 13, her brothers married and went their separate ways. The following year her father died. "After that it was just my mother and I, and we had no way to get around. I started having trouble in ninth grade getting along with other kids. From the time I was in first grade, I had trouble getting along with other children."

The school-yard slights of other kids cut Lori deeply, and she relied for companionship on one or two girls who also felt like outsiders. Brown-eyed with shiny, copper-colored hair, Lori tends to be overweight. "The others were into groups and so popular. I was nonexistent to them. I couldn't do any after-school things like sports because we didn't have any transportation. I had to go right home on the school bus. I finally lost interest in school, in everything, right after my father died."

Lori now views those years from her own perspective as the mother of a 17-month-old daughter, Alexa. Alert and curious, Alexa is a well-behaved youngster and quite obviously her mother's consuming joy and interest. Lori lives in a roomy two-bedroom trailer that she and Alexa's father, Nelson, share with her mother. There's a car in the driveway, and in the backyard a line full of baby clothes billows in the March wind sweeping across the rolling countryside. Lori's whole being radiates the happiness she never knew as a child.

"Ninth grade was a combination of becoming a teenager and losing my father. As a teenager I wanted to get out more and do things. I just felt trapped. And my mother and I started fighting a lot because we had no way to go anywhere. She went to work and came home, and I went to school and came home. After a while, I just stopped going to school because I couldn't get along with the kids, and I'd lost my father, and I felt like I wanted to give up. I didn't want to do anything with my life anymore."

About midway into tenth grade, Lori's guidance teacher mentioned the Community School to her. A short time later, Lori received notice that she was going to be held back a year. But she was skeptical about going to school in Camden. "I sort of liked the idea of getting out of Back Cove, but then, again, to think that I would be all the way over in Camden and not be at home. I was just afraid I was going to miss something, even though I really wasn't. It was really a big change."

When the guidance teacher took her to the C-School for the interview, Lori made up her mind: She didn't want to go to the School. "I walked in and thought, 'I'm going to be living with teenagers. Maybe that will be a little hard since I've just gone through all the trouble in school.' I decided I didn't want to go really. But then I went back home for a while and thought it over. 'Maybe that's a good idea because I'm stuck here, and if I stay here, maybe I won't do anything with my life.' So I decided to go."

She entered the fall term, 1985. One of her brothers drove her to the School, and when she looked at the other students, she thought, "Don't leave me." Lori didn't like the School at first. She found it hard to adjust to a totally new environment and to share a room with two other girls. "I always had this complex where I'm not sure if people like me, and I thought they didn't like me. That was kind of a hard thing to get used to."

At first she didn't want anything to do with academics until she realized she would not have to study all day and that each student had an individual tutor. Finding a job, being responsible for getting up in the morning, and going to work on time were new challenges for Lori. She got a part-time job at a day-care center and again wasn't sure she wanted to do it. She had never had a job before, but after a short time the job began to work out well for her.

"I got to know more people. I got out. I worked with a bunch of children, and I kinda liked it because I got along well with everybody there. I felt good because the kids really liked me, and it felt really nice to be needed somewhere and wanted." She particularly enjoyed the friendship of a co-worker, a woman somewhat older with whom she shared much in common.

Quiet by nature, Lori maintained her reserve at the School and had few behavioral problems. She had never tried drugs or alcohol, but when she saw students at the School doing it, she tried it too. "I was about halfway through the term when I decided I didn't like any of that stuff. That's when the kids began to think that I was square more or less, and I didn't get along with them quite so well." They went without her on their free time, and once again Lori felt left out. "I remained friends with them, but I wasn't real close."

Camping trips presented another unknown challenge. "There was a little bit of me saying I didn't want to do that, but there was a lot of me saying, 'Yes, I do. I want to see places. I've never been anywhere.' But I knew I had to do it if I wanted to get my diploma and feel I had made something of myself. It was something I had to do." The School's annual trip to Boston was a revelation to Lori. She had never been out of Maine, and just the drive itself—the changing scenery—was exciting. "The museums, Harvard Square, watching people like you see on TV. It was a little scary to see people all around us."

Looking back, Lori realizes, "The toughest thing for me was breaking away from home. Even after a couple of weeks I wanted to stay, but I missed home terribly." She also recognizes some truths she was too young and unhappy to understand at the time. "Sometimes my mother and I didn't get along very well. But I think part of that was just being stuck in the same house together, and becoming a teenager, you get rebellious. She was having a hard time dealing with my father's death and so was I. I really needed to get away."

The lesson she learned from the Community School was that she could make more of her life, be what she wanted to be. She had once played with the idea of suicide but never attempted it "because I didn't have enough guts to. But after I started going to the School, I forgot totally about that. I thought, 'I'm going to earn my diploma, and I'm going to grow up a little bit and learn how to handle life too.'"

After graduation Lori was reluctant to leave. She stayed around Camden for a while and worked at the IGA. "It was like leaving a home that I had lived in forever, and I knew I wasn't going to be able to go back. To this day I wish I could go back and do it all over again. And I would. I'd give anything to do that again."

She went back to Waldoboro, and a friend from the School stayed with her while they looked for work and drove around Maine. By then she had her license and a car—another major accomplishment. Lori had never dated, but soon after she got home, she met Nelson on a blind date arranged by a friend. They started dating, and after a couple of years they began living together.

For the first few months they moved about a bit until Nelson found a job in the Waldoboro area. Lori was pregnant by then and wanted to raise her child where she grew up. "We decided that when we feel like we're ready to get married, we will. My brother got a divorce, and it looks like an awful painful thing. So we're giving ourselves plenty of time to see if we want to spend the rest of our lives together. And so far, it looks pretty good."

Lori likes to tell stories to Alexa, simple little growing-up stories for young children that she wants to write in book form. "I love books, and she loves books, and I think that would be kind of a neat thing. Little stories, little pages. Some of them are disciplinary type things—saying 'please' and 'thank you' and sharing with other children."

Although she says she's "not good" with art, Lori has taught herself to use a 35 mm camera and is perfecting her photography using Alexa as a subject. Sometimes she can get a shot of deer or coyotes in the back field.

Lori's days are full and happy. She has met new friends through Nelson and renewed friendships with the young people she grew up with. "I'm a lot more sociable now." That, for Lori, covers a long, hard trail.

Peter Clement

"I have just about everything I want—got a good job and a happy family, everything I want." Peter Clement is one of a rare minority. Not many 24-year-old men in Eastport, where depression is chronic, can make that claim, much less a young man who spent most of his growing years on the adjacent Passamaquoddy reservation.

From his seat at the kitchen table, Peter can take in at a glance the big open living room of his trailer home, the long deep-cushioned couch where his wife, Dori, keeps their three young children—Rachel, 6 months, Peter, Jr., 3, and sister Lindsey, 5—amused while their father is being interviewed. Dori, a slender young woman with a mass of dark hair, grew up in Eastport, attended the University of Maine, and is the accountant for the tribe.

Peter has experience in a variety of fields. He worked as a carpenter, was a state-certified fire fighter, and served on the reservation police force where he is a reserve officer. When an opening in shipping and receiving at a local electronics plant was announced, he applied and got it. Now he takes inventory and does all the computerized scheduling of orders and shipping for customers all over the world, communicating with people in Italy as well as Japan.

"I've been in computers since grammar school, always been interested in computers. I'm still getting better at 'em." He works five or six days a week, sometimes Sundays, yet his broad full features radiate pleasure as he marvels once again at his good fortune. "I've got everything I want— a new trailer, new truck...."

Peter moved about a bit while he was growing up. He lived in Connecticut for a time and then on the Micmac reservation in Quebec with his father's tribe. Here he was taught French as well as Micmac in the first and second grade. But 15 years ago he returned to the Passamaquoddy reservation, where his mother grew up, and went to the Raferty School from fourth to eighth grade.

"I was a hellion. I was always getting expelled." Peter's problems escalated when he went to the public high school in Eastport. "I did a lot of crazy things I've kicked myself in the butt for. I skipped school. I used to drink, smoke, the whole shebang. I got expelled in ninth or tenth grade, went to Lee Academy, a private school, for a year, and got expelled out of there."

After he returned to the reservation, he got into trouble and was arrested and put on probation. "I was supposed to serve jail time, but they suspended it and gave me community work here instead." One of his counselors referred him to the Community School, and he entered the fall, 1985, term graduating the following spring.

Peter made up his mind with little outside persuasion. "I just decided I better go. I wanted to get a job and start working and earn things that I wanted. Because I come from a poor family and there's a lot of alcohol involved in it, I wanted things I never had. I figured the only way I could do that was go out and work for them."

He got a job at the Dragon Cement plant which the tribe owned at the time and worked there his whole term at the School. "I knew I'd get the job; made a few phone calls to the governor." And, laughing, "It's good to have connections."

Peter has good memories of the School. He feels he adjusted to the rules although he was put on probation for drinking once. A natural outdoorsman, he hunts and fishes and canoes in season, so camping trips were a natural. "I was ahead on my work hours, never late on my rent, and academics were no problem whatsoever. You see, I've got it up here," tapping his head. "It was just applying it. I was young and foolish, that's all.

"The only thing that slows me down is cigarettes. I don't smoke dope, haven't since I was back in Lee. I drink now and then. The School was a help. It made me fend for myself—work, pay rent, cook for myself—the real world. It helped me quite a bit, or I probably wouldn't be here today."

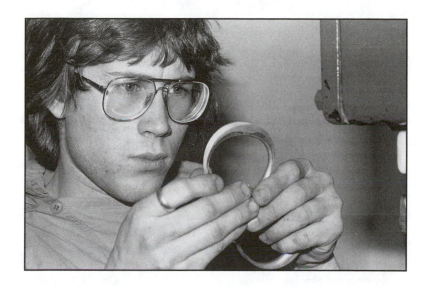

Luke Sunde

Unlike most young people in their early twenties, Luke Sunde has not held a variety of jobs. Aside from a season raking blueberries, he has worked for two jewelers since he was 16 making and repairing gold and silver jewelry. He enjoys his work and has become a skilled craftsman.

Nothing else in Luke's life approaches this degree of constancy or commitment. His frenetic shuttling from New York state to Maine throughout much of his elementary schooling found him in a different school for each quarter of the seventh grade. The moves were dictated in large measure by his parents' separation during the time and their uncertainty about where they wanted to be.

"My father read Thoreau when he lived in New York City, and he made a couple of trips to Maine. And that's where he wanted to go. My parents were the back-to-the-land hippie group. That was their whole trip." Although Luke has a half-sister and two half-brothers, they are much older, and essentially he was raised in an only-child environment.

He spent his early years with his parents in Trescott, a small downeast Maine community. Because he was slightly dyslexic and had difficulty reading, his parents took him out of the local public school and taught him at home for fourth and fifth grades. "I learned a lot those two years, a lot more than I learned in the school."

He went to high school in Machias, Maine, his freshman year, then to Nottingham Academy in Syracuse, New York, his sophomore year while he lived with his father. "It was sort of different going from Maine schools because there, if you've got a relatively retentive brain, you can go through high school and never ever do anything. In the New York school system, they're tougher. You don't have to go to class if you don't want to. Consequently, I didn't do very well. I still passed most everything because I sort of felt obligated and went in for the important tests. I always did well on those. I passed everything but English and French. Then I decided I didn't want to deal with high school, and I wasn't dealing with my father and stepmother very well, so I moved back to Maine, and I decided I couldn't live with my mother either."

Luke knew he had to finish high school "because it seemed like the convenient thing to do." His mother had heard of the Community School and encouraged him to look into it. A family friend, who was a jeweler in Camden, offered Luke a job if he could find a place to stay. Luke was accepted after being interviewed at the C-School and started working at the jeweler friend's the next day. He worked there throughout his school term and for six years following his graduation in March, 1986. He now works at his craft with another jeweler in the area.

"It was a phenomenally smooth transition for me. I'd saved up my money before I graduated and rented an apartment, so I just moved my stuff in while I was still at the School. Graduated on Friday and the next Monday went right back to work.

"Actually, the whole term was phenomenally simple. If you just follow the rules and do what they say, it's a breeze. It is showing you that there are certain priorities in life, and you gotta set your priorities. If you want to smoke dope, you can go out and do those things. You just have to have clean time, which is the same in the world. You can't go to work stoned. It just doesn't work that way."

In some respects Luke has never left home. He got settled early in a trade where the door was opened for him. He seems able to mesh his transmissions easily. But his control behind the wheel of a car has not gone all that smoothly. Luke's "penchant for pushing the limits" has wrecked a dozen of his cars and cost him money in fines and property. "I've decided now I want to get slow vehicles."

Luke often stopped by the School after he graduated. "It was a good place to go. It felt good to go there." Now he feels the School "has changed for the worse. It seems to have gotten a lot more disconnected from the students. It doesn't seem to be as warm a place. It was more a family, and now it's more like it's a job."

Nonetheless, he looks upon his time at the C-School as a good experience. He cites the everyday business of learning to budget money, pay bills, and take responsibility. "It taught me a good bit about communal living. I was very bad at it; I still am, but I'm better now than I was then. Living with people in general, dealing with their personalities—it taught me to look at what I was doing and how it interacted with other people. I learned social skills. It was a positive experience."

Rob Golgano

The village of Montville, Maine, is little more than a tree-shaded bend in a country road marked by a few white clapboard houses and a steepled New England church. "Nice? Not when you're a kid from the Jersey shore. It's a culture shock."

Rob Golgano looks back to his 9-year-old self transplanted to his mother's native turf where there was no place to skateboard but the county road. The school housed kindergarten through twelfth grade in the same building, in itself a jolting new experience. "My twin brother and I went to elementary school in Jersey and never saw each other all day. Both of us were pissed at moving up here. The whole school system was about one year behind, so I didn't have to do anything to pass because I'd been taught it the year before. I got in a lot of trouble being bored, acting out. A bunch of us were in school to have fun, raise hell all the time"

His mother worked in a town some distance away and left for work before the boys went to school. The shining light in his school experience was a junior-high teacher who tried to help him. "She was the best I ever had in my whole life." Even so, he started doing drugs in junior high and was suspended several times. He got through his freshman year in high school but had to drop out or be expelled when he was a sophomore.

"My mother wasn't happy about it. But I was 16, had my license, the use of her car, and a girl." Rob had heard about the Community School and tried to set up an interview before he dropped out, knowing he would need a diploma to do anything. He was commuting to a restaurant job in Camden, and after he was interviewed, he called the School every week hoping to be accepted. If not, his only choice was to go back to public school as a freshman.

His persistence paid off, but he felt the loss of leaving his freedom behind more than he expected. He kept quitting and changing jobs during the term, skateboarded a lot, got behind in social service and work time, and slipped in his rent payments. Then he got an internship at the Montessori School. "It was the only job that I liked to go to that I ever had in my life."

Rob felt he had total control of his drug problem although he continued to deal while he was at the C-School. One of his requirements for graduation was to see a counselor once a week. "Once I got my job and decided I wanted to stay at the School and get serious, I went from getting into trouble to not doing anything wrong. I caught up on my rent. I worked all the time, even weekends. I got serious about it because I had to or I would be thrown out. I worked with kids at the day-care center. I really love little kids."

Graduation was a photo finish. The last three days of school Rob was on drug and alcohol probation which he managed not to break. He worked until an hour before graduation to pay the last $50 of his rent.

Rob was 16 when he got out of school, and when his father offered him a job in New Jersey delivering insulation at $300 a week, he grabbed it. He often put in 60 to 70 hours a week. He played—partied and skateboarded—as hard as he worked and burned out. The next several years he fell into a pattern of working and living with his father in New Jersey in summer, then working in Maine in winter. "I had trouble tolerating jobs for very long—six months maximum. I'd usually take jobs just for the money. Half the companies I worked for I was the youngest guy there driving a truck. The whole society was geared to making money. I was sick of it. I didn't want to play the game anymore." He was also involved in a number of alcohol-related accidents. "Every time I'd drink, I'd get in trouble and end up in the hospital or in jail, once for five days. I paid everything I earned for two months in fines."

Rob moved back to Maine and shortly after hit a tree at 65 mph on a three-wheeler. After intensive care and a long recovery in the hospital, he went to rehab. It was three months before he was back to normal. Now alcohol and drug free, he feels he can go back to work with children once more. "Before, my use was too bad. I had enough dealing with my own life to help little kids through a crisis."

He keeps in touch with his parents better than he once did, and he also touches base with the Community School when he's in the area. He looks upon his term there as the "first thing I ever did for myself that I completed. That was a big thing. I think it prepares you much better for the 'real world' than high school does. You're living in the 'real world'—you got to work, pay rent, share chores. When you live in a house with seven other people just like you, you're learning something."

Aaron Schmidt

Aaron Schmidt moved with his family from Rhode Island to Aroostook County when he was 12 years old. He attended Presque Isle High School where he sang bass in the chorus for four years and was chosen for Maine's all-state chorus. His father had taught him to play chess when he was just four years old, and all through high school he was number one on the chess team. He liked poetry and wrote some on occasion. When school closed for four weeks during potato harvest—the major crop in Maine's huge northern county—Aaron joined other youngsters picking potatoes for 50 cents a barrel. In the classroom he had a remarkable ability to grasp subject matter quickly and pass tests.

"All I'd have to do was hear something once, read it once, and then I knew it. I took algebra, trigonometry, business math, accounting—I really like math. I think I had a 98 test average. But my homework average was zero because I never brought a book home. I kinda made my own rules. If it was a nice day, I'd skip class. So that was my problem."

Aaron has indulged a lifelong love affair with the wheel, particularly old-model cars. During his senior year in high school, he bought a motorcycle and owned an old junk car that he was trying to fix up. To help pay for it all, he worked at three part-time jobs after school.

"Like if I worked until 2 (a.m.), I'd go into school next morning and visit with my friends for a while, and we'd take off for a couple of periods. At that point, school didn't mean that much to me. I was too much into having a good time, trying to fool people, trying to outsmart them. All that time all I was doing was outsmarting myself. I look back at all the mistakes I made. If I could take it all back, I would in a second."

Aaron had been forewarned that he was headed for trouble. He had ignored detentions and had been suspended several times during his senior year. When he didn't show up for detention one night because he had to work, he had bucked authority one too many times and was expelled two months before graduation.

"My mother was real upset about it. And at the time I was kinda upset 'cause I wasn't allowed on the school grounds at all, and all my friends were going to graduate. So I didn't do much of anything."

He drove a trailer truck for a while delivering potatoes around New England and the mid-Atlantic states as far south as Virginia. He continued basic training with the National Guard but got out with an honorable discharge before his two-year hitch was over.

"I started hanging around with different crowds, drinking real heavy—even stopped playing around with my friends, basically. We stole some Ski-Doos, and the day before I was supposed to go to court for the Ski-Doos, we burned a guy's car."

He was fined and put on probation for the Ski-Doos. When it came to the car, Aaron had the choice of time in jail or pleading guilty to arson, a felony. Rather than have a felony on his record, he went to jail for thirty days. Before he went to jail, however, he got in a fight that proved to be a life-altering experience.

Aaron is a stocky man, built square and solid. He has a strong face with even features and a level, no-nonsense look in his eyes. It is easy to imagine that he would be a tough opponent in any combat.

"I got drunk one night and saw my ex-girlfriend, and she started giving me a hard time. So I started to leave, and she didn't want me to drive—I was falling-down drunk. Two guys that were there started with me, and two more of them came in. I'm pretty capable. I have a brown belt in karate. Somebody grabbed me from behind, and I turned around to swing at him, and I twisted my whole knee, all the cartilage and ligaments. The fight was over right there. So I had surgery on my leg.

"When I was in the hospital I realized what was going on with me: I had DT's. And I called up one of my neighbors—an alcoholic—and said, 'Is there an AA meeting around?' She said 'There's one right in the hospital.' So she came down, and I started going to AA."

Aaron heard about the Community School from a brochure his probation officer gave him. He liked the sound of the School, went to Camden for an interview, and was accepted. As soon as he got out of jail—which had been postponed during his recovery—he went home to Aroostook County for about ten days before moving to the School. He never moved back.

"My mother moved down here six months after I did and got remarried 'cause my father died when I was seven. She made a promise to my brother and sister and I that she'd keep us together and raise us, and she did a pretty good job by herself.

"When I come down here, I was trying to deal with my drinking, and I wanted something better. I wanted to get away from the nowhere life-style. Up there all you gonna do is go out and party or work in the potato field or work in the woods, and that's basically the three choices. So when I moved down here, I set my mind to doing it. I had the academics licked, no problem, and the rent. And I broke the hours' record for working 'cause I got a job the first day I was here.

"I have a problem with alcohol. I would consider myself an alcoholic, I guess. I can't stop when I'm drinking, but I can go six months or a year without drinking."

Learning to deal with anger and control his temper also presented problems for Aaron at the C-School. In one Group Rap he had his driving privilege pulled. "That was the only thing I ever got busted for while I was there. Me and cars—it's just an obsession." In a rage Aaron stormed out of the School, went outside, and demolished his car with his bare hands, splitting them open in his fury. "I've dealt with that—my anger," he says quietly.

For all his masculine toughness Aaron admits to feeling insecure about being alone. "If I'm not in a relationship, I have a real insecurity. It's a month and a-half since I broke up with a girl. We tried it three years. Three months after we started going out, she was pregnant, so we had our baby girl, and she's a little over a year old now. We broke up two, three weeks after her first birthday, and I moved out."

When time hangs heavy and lonely thoughts set in, Aaron travels back roads, ever on the alert for a classic car or some elusive part he's been trying to find. "It relaxes me and excites me." He's had more exciting if not unnerving times with automobiles.

"I have a heavy foot. When I came down here, I had sixty-nine points against my license—lost my license five times. Now I have eight. It was nothing for me in Presque Isle to be doing 110 without my lights on a back road, playing tag with somebody else doing the same thing, and drinking. Now I kinda value life a little more, value other people's lives.

"You gotta be happy with yourself before you can do anything, and that's one of the things you learn here (the Community School). The term after mine I was up here almost every day. I basically talked to Bob (Dickens). Bob was my one-to-one. I get along with him real well.

"I liked the School extremely. They taught me to see myself, see what I could be. This is the first thing that I accomplished all the way through. I graduated. I succeeded in what I set out to do. Even with karate I didn't finish. I set out to be a black belt, and I only got brown—a step below, but it's not quite there. Even in the Army, I got out just before my time was up. I got out just before high school was out.

"Now that's the way my life had been before C-School. I was telling myself I could outsmart everybody by proving I could do it, but not finishing. Here I proved that I could do it, and I finished. They taught me how to do that. I couldn't do it without them. The staff have a strange way of being your friend and your teacher.

"If a student comes here, obviously they have problems—not always but usually. And they learn about themselves. I think if you toss aside all the academics, this would still be a great school."

Jodi Thomas

For the first time since her bright young world collapsed in eighth grade, Jodi Thomas is excited about school—but now it's over art classes at a university rather than finger paints and crayons. Gone are the years when she never wanted to see school again and when as a 20-year-old she stashed her paintings out of sight in her Portland apartment. Jodi is completing work toward a Bachelor of Fine Arts degree in visual and performing arts at the University of Maine's Farmington campus and plans to do graduate work in art therapy.

"I think it was the divorce," Jodi says of the years everything "went downhill." Jodi's two older brothers and her older sister were getting married and leaving home during that time. She had enjoyed growing up in Bangor in a big family. Now only she and her younger brother were left, and her parents were breaking up.

"It was really hard. I thought I was losing touch with the world. I was sad and depressed all the time. I went to sleep a lot and stayed home from school. My mother tried everything to get me out of the house and go to school: I was going to see doctors, going to a nun at a hospital to see if I was sane, and getting tested to see if I was slow. I was none of those things. Yet I wanted to be different in a way because I didn't want to conform to what people wanted me to do."

She went to school so little in eighth grade that she had to go to summer school to make up the work. This was a drastic change in attitude in little more than a year. Jodi had loved kindergarten and elementary school, especially the fourth and sixth grades. Then in ninth grade she moved around to five different schools. "I was sick of seeing the same old people everyday. I didn't like my classmates. I was on a hate trip." Meantime, her mother remarried, and they left the house that had been home for a long time.

Jodi turned to punk rock. She dressed only in black with spike-heeled boots, miniskirts, and a Mohawk haircut. She moved in with a friend in Hampden on the outskirts of Bangor and transferred to Hampden Academy. Here she found people more "open-minded" and for the first term did quite well. Her mother's marriage was not working out, and she moved to Hampden where Jodi could live with her again. It was a financial struggle for the family, and to make matters worse, Jodi got in with the "wrong crowd" of punk rockers she met in Orono.

"We started drinking, smoking marijuana, even taking acid, but only on weekends. Then I got this bad attitude. I didn't want to do anything that anyone expected me to do. I stopped going to school, and I was doing fine. I told myself, 'Nothing is right, nothing is right.' Jodi was midway through tenth grade when she dropped out. A friend who had dropped out of school in Orono had applied to the Community School and told Jodi about it. She sent for information and called for an interview.

"So I went down there with my Mohawk and everything and the kids staring at me, but I didn't care. I was really hoping to get into the School. I liked what it said in the brochure—work, pay rent, go to classes. I liked that responsibility. But I don't think I was straight about a lot of my interview. I remember Bob (staffer Bob Dickens) asked me if I had been drunk, and I said 'no' because I thought it would incriminate me if I said 'yes.' I was told to go home and think about it and if I really wanted to go to the Community School, to call back. I called as soon as I got home."

Jodi had just turned 17 when she entered the spring term in April, 1986. Although she continued to drink during the two-month interval after her interview, she did not drink or do drugs at the School. "The day I left to go to the School, I picked up smoking cigarettes, my vice to have, and cut off my Mohawk. I thought I'd better shave it off to get a job. It was really, really short hair." But she got a job at the first place she applied.

The term was a "real growing experience" for Jodi. After the initial adjustment to getting along with other students, she enjoyed the School, her job, and the camping trips. She had always liked poetry and books and music—she plays flute—and read a lot while at the School. Studies posed few problems except for math—formerly her best subject—which took three tries to pass. When she got her diploma, she felt she "had done something wonderful."

After graduation Jodi moved to Portland, where for the next few years she worked at several jobs including one as assistant teacher at a day-care nursery. It involved long hours and responsibility, and she loved it. She took a course in early childhood education through the University of Maine's televised curriculum and studied art in Portland's adult-education program. She began to realize that what she wanted most was to find the right college and continue her studies. After a couple of years at Farmington, she dropped early-childhood education for a BFA in Visual Arts with an ultimate goal of art therapy.

"I knew the world isn't all peaches and cream when I went to the Community School, but I learned a lot about myself there, about other people, what to expect in the world. You have to get out there and work for what you want. I am grateful for going to the C-School. But it's just for some people. We were all one big relationship. We had to communicate and work together. I think I learned to love and accept people and accept myself. I think I really grew up in a big way."

Mike Owen

For years Mike Owen has struggled with a yearning to belong and a tendency to remain aloof. If he were to pinpoint a time when he became aware of this conflict, he would likely say the fifth grade. That was the year his family moved to Calais, some distance from the small Aroostook County town where he grew up.

Calais is a border town connected by bridge to New Brunswick, Canada. The steady flow of traffic through the town—daily cross-border trade, truckers, and tourists—energizes a tempo in the community that is alien to towns even a short distance away. The transition didn't come easily to Mike. He could not identify with any of the peer-group cliques in the school and felt like a castoff from the start.

"I didn't want to belong to any type of group and be stereotyped or categorized by what they did, either the drinkers, smokers, jocks, or honor-roll students. I never had a problem making friends even when I was in the Navy. Down here I didn't want to shut myself out from other people in order to fit into a certain group. I wanted to be not only accepted but to have the things that I liked without having the group influence me."

Mike is a slightly built young man with red hair and fair, freckled skin. He lives with his parents and younger sister in a Cape-style house on the main highway just outside the town proper. His personal space in this house is the small upstairs bedroom where everything is in its place, uncluttered, the bedspread stretched taut as though ready for inspection on a moment's notice.

Mike's desk is in a corner of the room where a new backpack, with a copy of J. D. Salinger's *Catcher in the Rye* secured behind a strap, is propped against the wall. He looks studious with his eyeglasses on and his books lined up before him. As he flips through a volume of Thoreau, it is obvious that he feels comfortable in his intimate, orderly surroundings. He likes to read and says he has become so engrossed with Tolstoy—now his favorite writer—that he read four of his works in the past three months. Robert Burns is his favorite poet, and lately Mike has tried his hand at writing poetry.

This might well surprise his former teachers in the Calais school system. During the fifth grade he did fairly well in school, but halfway through the sixth he began to get failing grades, a pattern that continued into high school. "They passed me just to pass me."

Mike began to consider dropping out of school. He didn't drink or hang out but intentionally began to miss the school bus in the morning. After the first ten or fifteen times he simply started walking the 5 miles to school. "I would walk straight to school, no detours. It was my way of rebelling. 'See, here I am, two periods late for class.' It would have taken me eight years to finish high school at the rate I was going. I did a lot of study on my own, sort of like educating myself."

Mike realized his school problems were creating a great deal of stress in the family. When he heard about the Community School through a former student, he decided to look into it. "I didn't want to try it so much as I just didn't want to go to school here."

Bob Dickens, longtime staff member, was Mike's first contact at the School. "When I saw Bob, I didn't know what to expect. Bob was in bare feet, and I think he was wearing a T-shirt. But I went in and there was a lot of like back-to-basics, sort of more homeyness than I thought it would be, a more simple-type setup than I thought."

In some ways Mike had a difficult time adjusting. He had a room by himself at first and didn't miss home or television—"none of the creature comforts at all." He recalls he tried to test the rules at the School but for the most part did not have problems with any of the students or staff. Dickens was his one-to-one staff person, and in retrospect Mike regrets one of his own attitudes at the time. "I wish I was as open back then as I am now. I think I shut Bob out of a lot of things. I like Bob."

Although he enjoys reading and poetry, Mike found writing his most difficult academic subject, particularly writing on an assigned topic. More important were the strides he made in his personal development. "I started opening up halfway through my C-School term. Before that I had become pretty closed off. When I'm here (Calais), I become withdrawn."

He felt he made friends at the School and was stimulated by the cultural climate in Camden which was greater than he found in his hometown. "I think a lot of the C-School's success is where it is located. There's a lot of particular culture in that area, a lot of different people who have their own identity and have their own likes and dislikes. It allowed me to be much more fluid in things I did. I can be myself and move inside the structure and just observe instead of being on the outside looking in."

Mike held several jobs during the term, the most rewarding being a clerical job at Hurricane Island Outward Bound in Rockland. After he graduated, Outward Bound gave him a free twenty-one-day course that involved camping in Baxter State Park, a canoe trip on the Penobscot River, and sailing in Penobscot Bay. In many respects it was the major experience in his life to that time. He did not return home after that but worked at Outward Bound for another month and signed up for the Navy.

For the next two years Mike was stationed in Connecticut then Seattle, where he left for six months in the Pacific. He saw Thailand, Australia, and the Philippines before returning home to Maine. But he was far from enchanted by the Navy. "I did not like the military at all. I thought they were very wasteful. There's a lot of propaganda in the military. I was very disappointed in it, but I did meet an awful lot of really good friends."

Soon after he got home, he enrolled in University of Maine branches both in Calais and Machias while waiting to enter UMO at Presque Isle. Mike credits the Community School for much of his social development. "It allows you to develop and strengthen your more positive character traits. That gives you respect for somebody else when you respect yourself. The way the School's set up, it makes it almost impossible for you to manifest traits which are undesirable. Everybody with a strong character influences the others."

Does he feel the School has any shortcomings? "If you'd asked me two or three years ago, I could give you a whole roll of 'em. I have a better feeling for the C-School than I did when I went there." As for getting in touch with the School, he pauses for a moment, then says, "It's a lot like leaving your friend and losing his address, then after a couple of years trying to find out where he is."

Rose Rapp

Rose Rapp would laugh if anyone called her "the Mom of the Community School graduates." Still, she is aware of her pivotal role among a coterie of former students for whom Camden has become a hub of their social and working life.

She works for a veterinarian who operates a mobile clinic in the area. Rose lives in town with another C-School graduate and keeps up with everything that involves staff and students at the School. Although she was a teenage parent herself and has tutored the parenting class, her devotion to the Community School is that of a daughter. She embraces each succeeding class as her sisters and brothers. At a recent graduation—she attends them all—Rose stood in the audience and told the graduates: "It is incredible to be able to go through and do what you have done. We are a family and always will be."

At 22 she is a good-looking woman with fair skin and reddish blond hair that hangs straight to her shoulders. She levels her brown eyes directly at you when she talks. There's no nonsense or pretense about Rose. She's as frank about herself as she is with other people. As an animal-loving kid growing up on a farm outside Portland, she hung around the neighbors' stable and rode their horses every day after school. In exchange she cleaned stalls and helped with barn chores. Over the years she became a competent horsewoman and competed in dressage events.

A combination of influences turned this wholesome way of going on its head. Rose dropped out of high school her first year and ran away from home. Almost overnight the country girl who loved hanging out with horses became a street kid in Portland. She was 17 when a near tragedy brought her to the Community School. Rose has learned a lot about herself in these six years and talks about it with uncommon honesty and perception.

From the time Rose was 6 months old, her mother worked as a nurse administrator in a Portland hospital. When she was 8, her parents were divorced, and her brother and sister went to live with their father for several years. "I never went to live with him. My father and I have major conflicts. We always have ever since I was a child."

Problems with school plagued Rose from her earliest years, due initially to a learning disability. Realizing she would have difficulty in public school, her mother held her back a year. Then Rose spent two years in Head Start. From elementary school on, her mother did constant battle with school authorities, and the records on Rose's psychological and performance tests began to bulge. "It was very frustrating for both of us," Rose says. "It made no sense to me why I couldn't sit down and do twenty questions on a paper. That made no sense to me whatsoever, but I couldn't do it.

"When I got in seventh grade, my attitude changed. I went to see a shrink, and I got a lot better. I started really working. I got an A-minus for the first time in my whole life."

The teachers liked Rose and realized the struggle she was making. But eighth grade brought a different set of teachers, less interested, Rose felt, and her grades dropped to C's and D's. She wasn't looking forward to high school, but she wanted to make it a "positive experience." The very first day, however, she got a rude awakening.

"I was outside talking with kids that I'd known most of my life. In the school society groups you'd probably call them the druggies or the burnouts. And the vice principal comes out, and he gives us this little speech like, you know, 'We don't really want you here, but we have to have you.' I don't remember exactly how he put it, but it was like 'If you do anything wrong, your ass is out of here.'

"I started skipping school about a month after I started. There's this one teacher who said, 'You know, Rose, why don't you quit? I don't want you here in my class.' And it was history. I love history, and I was so psyched to take that class. But my math teacher, he pissed me off so much that I did well. It was hilarious. But I was sick of it. I dropped out after five or six months."

Rose was 16, a couple of years older than the average high-school freshman because of her late start. She tried without success to find jobs. Then one night walking down the street of her hometown, she struck up a conversation with a boy who asked her to go to a party. Rose said, "Sure, why not?" They wound up for the night at someone's place in Portland, and Rose stayed there six months.

"The guy I was living with—there was nothing going on, I was just living there—was a dealer. I never did drugs. The hardest thing I ever did was caffeine pills, and I smoked some dope for a couple of months. I drank for a little while, but I never got drunk. I was on the street. I was considered a street kid. I used to live, you know, by my boyfriends. You really wouldn't call them boyfriends. They were just guys I went to bed with."

Shortly after Rose turned 17, events took a radical turn. During a get together at her place one night, a friend who had a gun drank too much, got in a fight with people in the next apartment, and in the melee someone was shot in the head. Two days later a gang of friends and relatives of the wounded man attacked Rose in a drug store and beat her bloody in the face.

At the hospital her mother rushed in and tried to put her arms around her. "I literally pushed her away. 'Don't fucking touch me.' I was in so much pain I couldn't stand having anybody touch me. Of course she didn't understand. She sees her baby, for chrissake just turned 17, push her away, scream at her, and she's got blood everywhere. I'm sure anyone would freak out."

Rose went back to her mother's to recuperate. During that time her mother tossed a Community School pamphlet her way, saying she had a patient with a head injury who had been to this school in Camden. "That's the only thing she could do. I was so self-destructive by that time that you couldn't suggest anything to me if it sounded like it could get me out of whatever I was doing."

Rose read the booklet and found it interesting. After her face mended, she went to the Community School for an interview with Tree Roth who later became a role model. "I always liked Tree; I respected her a lot." Rose was accepted a couple of days later and entered in mid-November, well into the term.

"I arrived with one helluva attitude. I'd seen pretty much everything and was damn good at what I did, and I walked out of there this meek little thing. It was incredible."

Rose settled into the School program, adjusting in some areas better than others. She got a job, pitched in with chores, and was "avid" about paying her room and board. She did her academics as well as she could and felt that the staff was understanding in their approach to her learning problem. The most difficult adjustment was to stop having sex. "When I was on the streets, I was pretty much addicted to sex. I didn't give a damn about drugs; it was sex."

No physical contact is one of the C-School's inalterable rules—no touching and no relationships with other students. "You couldn't go in other people's rooms, and I was always in the boys' rooms. I set a large punishment for myself. I said, 'If I get caught in anyone's room three times within the next week, I get kicked out.' And Tree said, 'Well, I think that's a little steep.'

"I had to learn how to deal with the sexual bit. I figured out—very vaguely, and it didn't really hit me until like last year, I didn't come out and say it—that my father used to beat me. I knew that he did, but I didn't realize how badly he used to do it. And I realized that I had a real big problem with the sex thing.

"The Community School was the best thing that ever happened to me. It turned my life around. That's what I needed. It was really incredible. I liked all the staff members. But Bob Dickens, Bill Halpin, and Emanuel were the first three men that showed me you could be nonviolent, you could communicate, and you could trust.

"I always had needed something or someone, I never knew what. It was interesting because I had always looked for it in the wrong places. But it started me in the direction that I needed to go to find what I needed for me. I'm still trying to find what I need and what I want."

Rose got pregnant during Christmas vacation, three months before her graduation. After that she went to live with her mother but called the School almost every week. After getting her license, she drove to Camden to visit the staff about once a month. The staff continued to counsel her and support her during her pregnancy and the legal arrangements involved in the adoption. Rose has visiting rights and keeps pictures of her blond, curly-haired daughter on her bureau. "If I didn't know the parents and pick out the parents and be able to go and see her, there's no way in hell I would have given her up."

In some respects Rose has not weaned herself from the Community School. It will undoubtedly remain a place of comfort and security for her, a home place for body and spirit. Now the youngest member of the Community School Board, Rose has assumed an adult role in the School that means so much to her.

Kshana Hitchings

Kshana means "thought" in Sanskrit, explains Kshana Hitchings. "Many vibrant thoughts derive from every breath taken." This bit of Indian philosophy he learned from his father, who was studying Sanskrit when he named his son.

Kshana, who prefers the last name, Roshi, his family name, is quite likely the most individual Community School graduate interviewed for this project. He operates on a tangent well outside the mainstream. His interests are eclectic, skirting the far side of inventiveness.

One area in need of fixing, he says, is the nation's transportation system. He plans to invent a perpetual-motion technology for transportation operated by counter-repelling magnets, no fuel required. The principle begins with the wheel, similar to an old wagon wheel mounted on an axle, with fan blades instead of spokes, its rim bounded by magnets with reverse polarity. The principle could be used in building jet engines or hovercraft.

Kshana wants to find a place to live and pursue such technological studies. "I'll know it when I see it. It'll probably be underground in a cave." At 21 he has had little experience in caving, but he professes to be "absolutely crazy" about caves. "They have the advantage of economy, even temperature, pure air, isolation, and protection."

Both the cave and the wheel tell much that is significant about Kshana's boyhood and the difficulty he had growing up in rural Maine. The wheel stems from his interest in science and science fiction and an innate ability to understand the inner works of mechanical and electrical equipment. "My parents used to go to the dump and bring me home a TV and whatever looked like top-of-the-line equipment. In my room there'd be circuits and wires going everywhere." At school he was acutely aware of being "different" and developed a shyness or fear of people that even now at 21 quite possibly lends appeal to the isolation and protection of cave dwelling.

"My father was the only person in town who had long hair. Because of that I was automatically a peace kid, and he was automatically a hippie. I was always teased and picked on and beaten up for it for no apparent reason. They were all rednecks."

Kshana, the eldest of four children, grew up in a small community on the downeast coast where his father had a tree farm and raised vegetables which he sold to Erewhon. When Kshana was four years old, he was run over by a car and received a severe head injury that left him with a slight speech impediment.

In the local school where total enrollment was about one hundred students in kindergarten through the eighth grade, "Everyone hated me. They put me in a migrant program and wrote me off as retarded. All I did there was sit like a bump on a log. At the end of the year the teacher would place me in the next class, and the next year they would pass me."

By the time he reached sixth grade, he refused to participate in school activities or do homework or anything that was required. His parents were reluctant to send him to another school because they didn't want to leave their land. Kshana says they now admit it was a mistake. "I could have told them back then."

Kshana became a loner. He would go survival camping in the woods, taking only a cigarette lighter, pocket knife, and a few fishhooks. "I'd build a somewhat waterproof shelter, make a bed out of dry leaves or boughs. It's surprising how you can keep yourself on just the floor of the woods." He prides himself on his physical dexterity and his ability to scale cliffs using only his feet and fingers.

In the eighth grade he was put on probation for three months. "I got involved with the wrong kind of people. They broke into houses, and I was with them. On the last day of probation I got in a fight with my father and got put on probation for three years." Kshana says he picked up a baby toy and threw it at a picture and broke the glass. This constituted breaking probation, he says, because "I was not even supposed to talk back to my parents. That was an act of talking back."

In the next three years, he says, "I kind of made a waste of my life. I became quite the alcoholic, then quite the druggie, then quite the recovery.

All I had to do was leave. Leaving is the beginning of recovery. I came here, quit drinking, and quit doing drugs."

It didn't happen quite so easily. Kshana heard about the Community School through mutual friends of the School in Stonington. He applied but was turned down because the School wanted him to go through a rehabilitation program first. "They didn't like me because I wasn't afraid to say, 'I like drugs and I'd do them if I see them.' But they quickly found out when I got there that I wasn't as bad as I sounded. In fact, I even quit when I was there." Kshana did not go to rehab, but he took a course designed for drug addicts at the Hurricane Island Outward Bound School.

After the twenty-eight-day course, "I just stood there knocking at their door saying, 'Let me in, let me in.'" He graduated in the spring, 1987, scoring high marks in math and science.

For a time he entertained the notion of shipping out on a freighter for New Zealand. He had spent some time fishing, lobstering, and musseling before he went to the C-School. He also did some urchin fishing, a lucrative export market opening up on the East Coast, but gave it up because the venture cost too much to get into on his own. Although he professes to "get along with anyone—the way I grew up, it was something that had to be done just to survive"—he still is wary of humankind. This was an area where he says the C-School did the most for him.

"I lost my fright for the general public world. I rarely saw people growing up, never hanging out in public. I always was around in public but would keep myself as much invisible from the general eyesight as possible. My shyness more or less vanished. I don't get offended. Now, I'm able to say, 'She's looking at me, so what? Big deal. I'm not scared.'

"The one thing I got from them which was important was the ability to have a face-off with the world. Years ago I was given a cabin on Isle au Haut, a small boat, and fifty-six lobster traps. That's enough for a little kid to take right off and make something of himself in that field. But I didn't. And there were two others. They were waiting for me to come and say, 'Let's do it,' and I didn't go. I just kind of let them fade away and melt off in the distance.

"The School gave me the ability to take the intimidations I felt for the world and turn that into 'Either we have a face-off, or we exist.' A face-off to me is a transaction of any sort. The School gave me the ability to deal with that—not be afraid to go out and do it, leave home. I was afraid at the time. The School gave me the confidence."

Gretchen Campbell

There was a time when Gretchen Campbell never thought she would be where she is—happy in work that had been a childhood dream. The horse-loving kid who wanted to be a veterinarian is a graduate vet technician from the University of Maine interning at the Cincinnati Zoo and Botanical Gardens. Her dark-lashed hazel eyes are alive with the excitement packed in her small frame as she talks about her work and plans to join the Peace Corps. Her words tumble in a torrent as she recalls the emotional hurdles along the way.

Just as in dressage competition, Gretchen's stride in life was to excel. "I was an overachiever. In seventh grade I was so worried that if I didn't get an A in everything, I wouldn't be accepted into vet school. It was an obsession. And it backfired. I wore myself out."

Gretchen went to public school in rural Fairfield, Maine, up to the eighth grade when she transferred to Oak Grove-Coburn, a private school. "I loved my freshman year. I was riding high and felt on top of the world. But you can't stay up there for long." Her obsession with school and success had blocked her recognition of problems at home.

"Life at home was increasingly difficult with an emotionally challenging mother and an alcoholic father. My focus to achieve above all got blurred, and my grades began to fall. Receiving poor grades was a strong signal that I was in the most painful and emotionally draining period of my life."

In her sophomore year, her father died not long after her mother's new husband died. Gretchen was living with her mother at the time, trying to cope with the emotional stress at home and her work at school. When her junior year started, she lost her motivation. Things that had been important lost their meaning. She began to feel so alone and isolated that she left impressions with her family that she was going to commit suicide. "I didn't want to die. I wanted a door leading out of the pain. I thought if I was persistent enough, someone would listen and offer me help."

She left school that Christmas vacation and voluntarily admitted herself into the psychiatric ward of a hospital. "I really wanted to get my life back in order. What I learned, though, was that my life had worth and meaning, but I had never learned the proper tools to see that. The hospital became the first stepping stone on the path to a happy and fulfilling life and the first of many healthier decisions on my own behalf."

Gretchen could not be discharged until she had a place to go. When she read the brochure about the Community School a counselor gave her, she said, "That's the last place I want to go. I'm not a high-school dropout. I'm fighting and working, and I don't feel as if I'm a loser." Pressed by doctors and counselors, she agreed to go for an interview.

"Right away I knew I wanted to go because of the people I met at the interview. It wasn't what I expected at all. They asked a lot of personal questions about my history, family, drug use, and sexual preferences. I knew by these open and direct questions they had my same philosophies. They seemed accepting of the fact that I had problems in my life and that I needed to be known as a unique and capable person. My biggest fear then became whether they would accept me."

Gretchen had been in the hospital three months and went directly to the School at the start of the spring term in April, 1988. "I loved the camping trips and the jobs I had throughout the summer. They made me feel alive and striving towards a goal again. What I got from the School was learning to live with other people—accepting them as individuals and the ability to communicate my needs to them. It worked out most of the time."

After she graduated, Gretchen went to Baxter State Park and worked until the end of November for the Maine Conservation Corps, a job she thoroughly enjoyed. She lived with her mother that winter and took adult-education courses to become a Certified Nurses Aide. She worked at a number of jobs to earn money, including a stint as a gas-pipeline surveyor in New Mexico. Back home she applied to a vet technician school in Colorado and a college in Vermont and was accepted, but she turned both down because she felt she couldn't raise the money.

Gretchen had always known that an academic environment was the best place for her. But a residual fear of failure inhibited her from entering college, and she used money as an excuse. "I thought that I had lost the motivation and strength I once had until I found the courage to enroll at the University. I credit the Community School with showing me that anything is possible if you conquer the fear and keep an open mind."

Gretchen tutored at the School for a semester and wants to stay in contact with it and work towards its continuance for others. "I believe the Community School was also a major stepping stone on my path of personal success, and right now I can happily say my path is reaching far into the big and bold horizons of tomorrow."

Amanda Moreland

Amanda Moreland had dropped out of five schools and was asked to leave a sixth before she learned she was not a golden child. The realization was as startling as the discovery that she was golden in the first place. Startling because she had a hard time making friends all her young life. During elementary school she felt more at home reading books and riding horses. Then at junior high in Camden, she suddenly found at 13 that she was very popular with both boys and girls. This was a heady new experience, and her school work suffered dramatically. "It threw me, and I didn't want to do as well in school. I was a cool kid. Cool kids don't do any algebra."

At the end of eighth grade, she went with her mother to Spain in connection with her mother's business. Amanda was enrolled in an English school where the teachers spoke French and Spanish and all the English students spoke French. Amanda spoke neither, and after two weeks she left. For the next five months she traveled with her mother around the country and didn't attend any school.

When they returned from Spain, they went to live in her grandmother's big rambling house in Boothbay Harbor. Instead of going back to eighth grade, Amanda was sent to Kents Hill, a private coeducational high school in central Maine, where she went right into the freshman year. She got through the year fairly well, but in her sophomore year, distracted by the death of her grandmother and the resultant disposition of family property, she didn't pick up a book.

"I was really caught up in being popular. I felt I didn't need to go to school. But I did need to do my algebra, and I was asked nicely to leave. I was totally shook. I cried all around the house. I was just blown away."

Amanda left Kents Hill with 3-1/2 credits for her freshman year and none for her sophomore year. The midyear semester was starting at the regional high school in Boothbay, and she was put in the freshman class. "I was 15 and going to school with 13- and 14-year olds. I didn't know anybody; I was the new girl. All those kids had been going to school together for years. It's a small town. They knew my grandfather was a doctor and I lived in a big house and went to a private school, so I was met with a little bit of aggression. I felt like an outcast."

Even going to the cafeteria for lunch was awkward because little groups of students habitually ate together in special places and she felt she didn't belong. Instead, she went to the library, explaining that she wasn't hungry, and got detentions for missing lunch. She soon lost interest in her classes because she had taken much of the work before, and she dropped out.

That summer she stayed home, worked in a local bakery, and connected with Kents Hill friends. Winter came, her friends left, and her boyfriend, an honor student at Kents Hill, went to Boston University. Amanda went back to high school in Boothbay, again as a freshman. "I should have been a junior. I just couldn't buckle down, so I dropped out again."

At that point her mother said she no longer wanted Amanda to stay at home. She went to stay with her boyfriend in Boston, but being underage and out of school with no job, she soon came back. Her best friend's mother offered her a place to stay at her house in Thomaston where she could go to Georges Valley High School. Amanda turned over her $25 a week child support for room and board and entered Georges Valley as a sophomore. She stood it for three months, and finally at her lowest ebb she called on her junior-high guidance counselor for help. He suggested looking into the Community School, just one street over from the junior high in Camden.

Amanda was familiar with the Community School from her junior-high years. "I was so cool and so hip, I'd walk by and say, 'oh, high-school dropouts.' And I was scared of it. Kids would hang out the windows and shout. I told the guidance counselor, 'That school's for dropouts.' And he said, 'You're a dropout, honey—more than once.' I was really scared, but I needed a high-school diploma."

She screwed up her courage and went over to the Community School where she talked with Dora Lievow, the co-director, who was in the kitchen cooking chili. She explained that she had dropped out and needed a chance. Dora set up an interview with a staffer two weeks hence. When it was over, Amanda went back to Boothbay to spend a long, lonely wait before she heard from the School. Her acceptance was based on two conditions: that she write a letter about a suicide attempt in junior high and take a nonviolence class. It had come out in her staff interview that Amanda had an explosive temper. "My mother and I would have fights. I'd throw things around. I smashed the front of a big Pepsi machine right down the street in Boothbay. I talked to the man who owned the store about it."

After she was accepted, she suddenly became excited at the prospect of going to the Community School. "I realized that I was getting more humbleness in my life." Amanda was 17 when she entered the fall term, 1988. The two-week trial period took intense effort adjusting to living in a small house with seven other students of different backgrounds and interests. "It was hard, but Bob Dickens, my one-to-one, gave me the Red Fox award for being able to make friends with other students and still hold my own ground."

Every week she met with staffer Buck O'Herin to talk about her anger and conflict resolution. "When I get into situations now where I can feel energy and bad feelings building up, I really do stop and think because I have the potential to do things. You cannot meet aggression with aggression. I realized it was a lot easier to get something that you want if you give something back, if you're not always trying to take something first."

Amanda got a job at a day-care center during the term. She was the first in the class to complete all her cooking and social-service requirements, and she won extra points simply following the rules. "The biggest problem was the physical-contact rule. I'm a very touchy person. I hug people. Everybody needs a hug, but physical contact means you can't brush up against a person or touch somebody's hand. I didn't understand. I had to write a paper on why they have a physical-contact rule. Think about it. Some people don't like to be touched. A lot of people come to the School who have been abused and have a reaction to being touched. So you have to learn to respect everybody's body space. You ask for a hug, which is something I never did before." She was put on probation, however, for reading the staff log containing teachers' notes about the students.

It had been a bumpy road from junior high, but at the end of the term, Amanda got her high-school diploma. "I was feeling really bad about myself when I went into the C-School. It gave me more of a feeling that I wasn't a failure because I had dropped out. I could start something and finish it."

The Community School:
An Intimate Form of Education

Although the stories in this book eloquently describe some effects of a Community School education, they do not give a clear picture of the program itself. In this chapter I have outlined the program's philosophy and design and the unique role of teachers within this context. Without going into a comprehensive list of our activities (for example, community service, art classes, and the relapse group are not covered), I have sketched a broad overview to give a sense of the education that the graduates in this book experienced.

As of 1993, 241 students and 34 teacher/counselors, consultants, and administrative assistants have participated in our experiment. Each of them would describe a somewhat different school.

Philosophy

Although the School's philosophy changes by degrees as teachers and students participating in it change, certain beliefs have remained constant over time:

Choice: Community School students experience education as a result of their choice to learn. Their internal motivation is the most important factor in determining their capacity to learn. We want our students always to be aware that *they* are responsible for applying to the program, attending it, and making a success of it.

Intimacy: Important lifelong learning occurs in a trusting and close community. The School is as near to family size as feasible to encourage the development of meaningful and sustaining relationships between students and staff. The roles of teacher and student must accommodate this emphasis on the relational.

Belonging: Most people need to feel that they belong to some human constellation, be it family, club, team, etc. One's ability to belong is determined by one's ability to trust oneself and others. The School is a place where students and staff can belong to and be a contributing part of an ongoing community, a community which will be accessible to them long after they have departed. The School places a high value on treating others within and outside of its community respectfully and nonviolently. Sharing this value is a prerequisite for being a part of the School's community.

Success: Many of our students need to feel successful quickly. The range of educational experiences offered is as broad as possible so that "nontraditional" students who are capable with their hands have as much chance to shine as "traditional" academically capable students. The School provides meaningful challenges to its students that lead to a culturally important credential: the high-school diploma. Achieving this degree establishes their competence in the present, supports their hope for the future, and increases their ability to reconnect positively with the larger community.

Survival Education: Learning takes place in the real world and is relevant to the students' needs and desires. The School prepares participants for life after graduation by helping them to learn and perform living skills essential for independent functioning. In this light, learning to hold a job, cook, clean, and pay one's bills are at least as important as studying a poem or solving an equation.

Rites of Passage: Students who drop out of school have lost a culturally sanctioned avenue into adulthood. It is crucial that all adolescents have a way to make this journey, especially those who have consistently perceived themselves as lacking competence and opportunity. With support and attention from their families, the School's staff, and their fellow classmates, students at the School can experience and celebrate this most important transition from teenager to adult.

Lifelong Learning: Just as children begin learning long before they enter educational institutions, they continue to learn long after they obtain their last degree. As a center for lifelong learning, the School is available to graduates at all stages of their postgraduate development. The opportunity for reconnection exists for every participant in the program.

Structure

Space: The Community School is housed in a three-story, two-family building on a residential street in Camden, Maine. On the top two floors are four student bedrooms, a music room, student lounge, bathroom, and the Outreach/Aftercare office. The ground floor holds a kitchen/pantry, a living room which doubles as a group meeting room, library, staff overnight space, a dining room which doubles as a classroom, and an office.

Each student shares a room with at least one other student. With a full contingent of eight students and one teacher, private space and house facilities are limited. Although students may not enter each other's rooms, they are free to come and go everywhere else in the house; it is their space while they attend the program.

Time: One of the program's most attractive features for some prospective students is the time factor. Given adequate academic skills and a strong desire to do so, participants can attain their diploma in six months. For 16- to 20-year-olds a six-month commitment is conceivable, especially when the result is a tangible, sought-after accomplishment.

Applicants are interviewed throughout the year. If an applicant is interviewed and found to be in need of academic, vocational, relational, or personal work, a preprogram is developed for him or her by the interviewer. Depending on the length of the waiting list, a candidate may have to wait up to a year to begin his or her residency.

Those who are accepted enter the School in groups of eight in April and October, finishing five-and-one-half months later in September or March. If a participant leaves the program during the first eight weeks, an appropriate candidate from the waiting list is accepted to fill the vacancy.

A quarter of our students complete the residency requirement and then finish other diploma requirements externally. With the assistance of our Outreach/Aftercare Program, two thirds of our external students finish within a calendar year of their term's graduation. Others stretch this completion period out for years.

Curriculum

Vocational: Work forms one-third of the School's curriculum. Students hold jobs in the community and are required to pay a portion of their room and board expenses from their earnings. At the beginning of each term daily classes introduce students to the basics of finding work and determining what their interests and capabilities are.

In the winter when jobs are scarce, the School runs its own internship program helping students to find work in nonprofit agencies and businesses where they can pursue a career interest or develop basic job skills.

A job in the real world which involves training and pay is an ideal education for experiential learners. Work gives students the opportunity to support themselves, to compare their preconceived notions of working with the realities of holding a job, to connect with the adult working community, and to develop a sense of themselves as economically independent.

Academics: The intent of the academic curriculum is to help students understand themselves as learners, to build their critical thinking skills, and to support their experience of themselves as capable and resourceful learners. In evening classes two to five community volunteers join the faculty to tutor individual students in six required subjects: math, science, social studies, grammar, writing, and English literature. Students are required to pass a standardized competency test in each of these subjects except writing. The pass/fail system is used in all courses.

Classes are completely individualized and self-paced. They emphasize building skills for some and studying areas of personal interest for others who do not need work on the basics. Regardless of a student's skill level, the classes are designed to be as relevant as possible to his/her current interests. When a student passes the core requirements, s/he and the teacher can create curricula and assessment contracts for advanced classes.

Interpersonal: Because the School has a residency requirement, each six months a new community of students and teachers forms. Students are given a respite from their home environments only to find themselves in a group that accepts and respects them as significant members but also requires them to take responsibility for their actions and to work on resolving personal issues which impede their progress in the program.

Living in a house with seven other teenagers and one or more faculty demands copious interpersonal skills from everyone involved. The School has developed several structures to facilitate this.

Weekly Group Raps, attended by all current students and teacher/counselors, are focused on self-governance and interpersonal relations. Discussions range from making individual disciplinary decisions (each participant has one vote) to processing a participant's or staff member's concern to solving a practical house matter. Group Rap is also the setting where the community extends its positive regard to the individuals that make it up.

"One-to-ones," advisorial dyads of one student and one teacher, meet at least weekly. The teacher acts as advisor, coach, advocate, and/or friend for the student for the entire term: The student brings issues to discuss and resolve dealing with everything from interpersonal conflicts with other staff or students to relations with his/her parent(s) to developing Group Rap proposals for "misdeeds" (rule breakings). The two primary purposes of these meetings are to establish a trusting relationship and to facilitate the student's progress through the program. Frequently the strength of this relationship fundamentally sustains a student's effort to complete the program.

A staff represents his or her "one-to-one" in staff meetings when individual program decisions are made and can be a crucial ally in Group Rap. Establishing and developing a healthy, helpful ongoing relationship with one caring adult provides a student with the confidence and experience to carry on other interpersonal relations; it also provides an important link to the larger School community.

Special Classes: The School offers a series of classes on relational skills. Conflict resolution and mediation, sexuality and self-esteem, and parenting are taught to everyone in formal academic seminars. Skills for resolving conflicts, working on relational issues, and parenting are identified and practiced.

For some students a specific course, such as anger management or assertiveness, is required as a condition of acceptance. These are taught in informal tutorials focusing on day-to-day events in the student's week. This curriculum flags the issue for students, teaches them to observe themselves, and helps them develop coping techniques to replace unproductive or destructive behavior.

Life Skills: Day-to-day household management is carried on by all students and staff. The ability to clean, cook, and maintain the premises is a graduation requirement. Several students interviewed for this book cited their responsibilities as being an important aspect of their education at the School. These chores allow them to have a quick success; they get credit for each task performed, immediately become a functioning part of the community, and learn fundamental living skills.

Although *cooking* is technically one of the chores, it has been elevated to a higher status since it requires more skill and time and has a dramatic effect on the community. Each student participates in a series of cooking seminars and has a tutorial as part of the curriculum. A student must cook six approved meals before graduating.

Our *physical-education* program combines camping, challenges such as ropes courses, and cultural activities. Trips are taken to natural areas of interest, metropolitan areas, and on occasion Canada. The aim of this program is to enhance students' enjoyment of the natural world, to help them learn recreational activities, and to show them how to organize and implement outings for family or friends.

A set of *"inalterable" rules"* form a framework for our behavioral program. These proscriptions include: no drugs, no violence or threats of violence, no sexual relationships between students, no weapons, no motor vehicles, automatic consequences for substance abuse, curfews, and the respect rule—no name calling, put-downs, or words intended to hurt.

Consequences for broken rules are proposed by the violator and voted on by the entire group of students and teachers during Group Rap. Students lose their voting privilege until they finish the consequence. The community may propose new rules or modify existing ones in Group Rap.

During each term participants develop a *postgraduation plan* with the Outreach/Aftercare staff. Included are the student's plans for work, further education, and living arrangements. Outreach/Aftercare helps students finish the program externally when they don't complete all its elements during their residency. Students who need help with college applications, job counseling, and personal problem solving can use the program regardless of when they attended.

The Teachers

Underlying many goals and principles of the Community School is a desire to have students and teachers treat one another as human beings. To a degree this means abandoning traditional educational and therapeutic roles. Teacher/counselors live on the premises with the students so that the variety and extent of their interactions can go much farther than in conventional schools.

The roles of a Community School teacher are a combination of parent, counselor, teacher, janitor, group worker, learner, camp counselor, and landlord. Likewise, a student is a worker, group member, learner, janitor, tenant, peer counselor, and teacher.

Curiously, a description of the affective, relational, and cognitive aspects of a Community School teacher's job is similar to the job description for good elementary school teachers. They relate first to the students and secondarily to the subject matter. They are generalists, capable of learning and teaching a wide range of subjects.

Community School teacher/counselors are often learning facilitators, helping guide students to what they want to know or need to know. Our teachers are frequently reminded that teaching and learning are not the same thing and not necessarily even related. People can learn without or in spite of teachers, and people can teach without anyone learning.

In this context being able to listen to students is more important than being able to explain information to them; being able to make students feel appreciated, accepted, and respected is more important than assigning them a grade for work done.

All teaching at the School is done by a team of teachers. Staff work in every aspect of the program and help each other to organize learning in all subject areas.

The faculty are skilled at paying attention to individuals, especially their one-to-ones. Counseling and reflective skills are critical. As educators they must balance the conflicting requirements of being supportive and maintaining a standard for how things, i.e., chores and class participation, need to be done.

Teacher/counselors also spend much time dealing with the real world—talking to employers, arranging community-service projects, working closely with parents, and finally folding those experiences into students' curricula.

Teacher/counselors find the time to engage students' questions, to talk personally, and to reflect on experiences with them—unplanned discussions where real learning takes place.

Stressing the relational, the extracurricular curriculum, and an ability to be flexible with class planning necessitates that the teacher/counselors be able to deal with a certain level of chaos continually; teaching and learning in the real world does not lend itself easily to the cleanly parsed and diagramed forms of the conventional curriculum.   —EP

Afterword

It never occurred to me when I began this book that I would discover a community of survivors or that I would come away with an inexplicable sense of kinship.

The Community School began during the years I was editor of the local newspaper. We covered its events and supported the School editorially during its legal battles involving the move to its present location. Over the years I came to know a number of C-School kids. They were a distinctive group in style and bearing, quite discernible from the students attending Camden/Rockport High School.

What I did not recognize at the time was the depth of their hurt. Later, as a tutor at the School, I caught glimpses of their personal struggles while we worked one-to-one on English and Social Studies in the regular night classes. The true burden of their lives did not hit home until their stories unfolded—some forty or more—in interviews for this book. Despite differences in age or year of term, a kindred bond of shared experience exists among them.

At an organizational meeting of the School's Outreach/Aftercare Program, I was struck by the instant camaraderie that surfaced, the easy familiarity of the group most of whom had met within the hour. They traded stories of cooking failures, camping trips, and Group Rap, the often painful Thursday night airing of personal and group grievances. In their banter, these former students unconsciously revealed that the School remains a constant in their lives.

A number of students interviewed had not completed academic work or settled accounts required in order to receive a diploma. Some view this with the affectionate intention of a family debt, one they expect to repay in time. And periodically they do.; several are studying to fulfill academic credits under the Outreach/Aftercare Program. At times I ached watching the dogged determination of two women in particular to get their diplomas. Out of school for eight or ten years, they struggled to recapture half-remembered studies in cramped households with young children underfoot. It took more than a year's commitment for each, but they did it.

Some question why the School, often a last resort for getting a high-school diploma, would kick out a student for coming in a minute late or not paying room and board. The Community School is not an academic grist mill for a high-school diploma. A relatively small number of students have been dismissed for repeated violations or unacceptable behavior. One of the students interviewed was allowed to return after being dismissed, then graduated and went on to college.

The Community School recognized early on that the dropout problem was rarely related to academics alone. In the interviews, students from every period since the School began revealed that the School deeply affected their wholeness as people. One student pointed out that kids who come to the School have known the worst by the time they arrive. What propels them to apply to the Community School is a gut-wrenching need to turn their lives around. "If you're ready to stop screwing around with drugs and start trying to live a halfway normal life, then you're ready to go to the C-School."

A decision to go to the C-School generally follows the stark realization of where they are and a barebones confrontation with themselves on what to do about it. The turning point for one was hospitalization after suicide attempts. For another, it followed violence, jail, and a terrifying bout with DT's. And for many, it followed years of abusive home life.

Often students hear about the Community School from a brochure given them by a parole officer, social worker, or substance-abuse counselor. "I liked the sound of the School" or "I knew it would be the perfect place for me" or "it sounded hopeful" is the consistent reaction to the message they read. It offered promise of a new start to kids who had known little else but failure and a devastating loss of self-worth. "I had no place else to go" was echoed repeatedly.

The public school system's handling of a number of these students points out a lack of sensitivity to and understanding of young people outside the mainstream on the part of teachers, guidance counselors, and administrators. One student walked out of high school for the last time when a teacher ridiculed her before a full classroom for skipping study halls and put her in a corner behind a room divider.

Another, talking with friends on the school steps the opening day, was told by a school administrator that the school really didn't want their kind but was obliged to accept them and followed it with the threat of explusion if they caused a problem.

"Responsibility" is the word most mentioned as the key element of the School experience. Former students time and again stressed the value of learning that responsibility to others and to themselves is an elementary fact of life. A graduate who earned money in grade school selling drugs on the Passamaquoddy reservation found out that responsibility involves "basic life skills that you don't learn in high school—like getting up in the morning, cooking, going to work."

It was interesting to find that students who once rebelled against any form of authority welcomed the security of discipline, indeed, came to recognize discipline as a form of love. As one young woman pointed out, the School "set limits when I couldn't." The fact that staff expected mature behavior and leveled with students as adults was for another graduate "one of the biggest things I was impressed about."

Others were strengthened because they had completed something they set out to do. "My first success," said one graduate, now in college. "It allowed me to complete something—start something and finish it" was a real achievement for another. One bright young man ticked off a host of goals thwarted by his failure to complete the final leg of the challenge. "This time I not only proved I could do it, I finished."

Not all students interviewed are doing as well in their personal and working lives as they might wish, or in some cases as had been generally expected. A number still struggle with their addictions. And many skirt an economic borderline with small children in crowded, often substandard, housing.

But a healthy number are attending college, are graduates, or are occupied in creative and fulfilling jobs. One young woman worked years in graphic arts and now has her own business with several employees. Another graduate whose future appeared hopeless when he entered the C-School now teaches his Native-American language in the reservation school. An early graduate overcame a severe addiction and now is a Phi Beta Kappa social worker counseling young drug users.

In these interviews I felt humbled by the students' unfailing openness, honesty, and self-awareness. They know who they are and have learned early to accept themselves without pretense. They freely opened the most painful periods of their lives to talk with me about the role the Community School played. I admire their courage in facing up to personal struggle without losing laughter and a buoyant spirit—and I am the richer for having known them.

—Jane Day

Endnote

The photographs of Kerrie Highhouse, Mark Sabatis, John Joseph, Debbie and Dennis Pearse, Terry Dolloff, and Aaron Schmidt were taken by the author, Jane Day; the others were taken by Maryanne Mott.

Jane Day has worked for radio, wire service, newspapers, and magazines for 35 years as reporter, feature writer, and editor. She lives in Camden, Maine, where she free-lances for regional publications.

Deborah W. Meier was the founder and teacher-director of a network of public alternative elementary schools in East Harlem and is currently the principal of Central Park East Secondary School, a New York City public high school. The schools she has helped create, serving predominately low-income African-American and Latino students, are considered among the best in New York City and exemplars of reform. She was the recipient of the 5-year Catherine D. and John D. MacArthur fellowship in 1987.

Emanuel Pariser cofounded the Community School in 1973 and has co-directed it since then. He has published articles, given workshops, helped organize national conferences on alternative education, and worked to draft legislation creating Maine's Office of Dropout, Truant, and Alternative Education.

Maryanne Mott began her career in photography only after her two children were grown. Most of her training has come over the past eight years from workshops in Montana and California where she lives and Maine where she visits often. She has exhibited her work in galleries in both California and Montana and her photos have appeared in a number of national publications.